MW00638377

# Cherish
## *the*
# Earth

# Cherish
## *the*
# Earth

*The Environment and Scripture*

## JANICE E. KIRK &
## DONALD R. KIRK

WIPF & STOCK · Eugene, Oregon

Wipf and Stock Publishers
199 W 8th Ave, Suite 3
Eugene, OR 97401

Cherish the Earth
The Environment and Scripture
By Kirk, Janice Emily and Kirk, Donald R.
Copyright©1993 by Kirk, Janice Emily
ISBN 13: 978-1-5326-1194-0
Publication date 10/31/2016
Previously published by Herald Press, 1993

*For our children, Ned and Amy,*
*and for all others*
*who would inherit the earth.*

# Contents

# Acknowledgments

THE CRYSTAL CLEAR WATERS of Lake Chelan lapped at the dock pilings as we climbed off the passenger ferry and trudged to the blue school bus. Moments later we wound up the road that followed Railroad Creek Canyon. Curiosity mounting, we journeyed on through maples and conifers. When the bus pulled out of the trees, the lodges of Holden Village lay before us. Beyond, heavily wooded slopes rose to snow-crowned peaks. The Glacier Peak Wilderness wrapped a blanket of beauty and peace around the Village.

But to the left, our vision was assaulted by an ugly scar of yellow earth—a gigantic mountain of mine tailings, flat-topped, with steeply sloped sides dropping abruptly to the creek. It cast a forbidding barrier across the mountains.

Living in Christian community for a time was a life-changing experience. Rising each morning to a landscape of such contrasts awakened within us the knowledge that humans can be a destructive or a healing force. We watched Holden Village deal with the problems of the environment, nurturing the earth in the midst of an old mining site. We resolved to be a nurturing force too. The natural world we loved and enjoyed was in need of help.

This book is a result of our sojourns at Holden Village. We are grateful to those who motivated, helped, and supported us: Cathie Elliott, who started us; our readers in the early stages—pastors Cliff Baker, Randy Yenter, and Greg Tyree; author David Douglas (*Wilderness Sojourn*, Harper & Row, 1987); Al Pitcher, who put us on the right track; our later readers—Sallie Nicholas, Carol Allen, Pat Bunselmeier; environmental science professor Mel Shuster, and Andy Jessen of Simpson College (Redding, Calif.).

We thank Cliff Westergren of the Christian and Missionary Alliance for his help. We appreciated prayer support from friends and colleagues. We also thank groups that responded to discussion material and slide programs, especially at Holden Village in Chelan, Washington and in the Neighborhood Church of Anderson, California.

Great appreciation goes to S. David Garber, Michael A. King, and the staff at Herald Press for their fine help in shaping this book into final form.

We hope this book will motivate Christians to care for the earth. Small enough to carry in a backpack, it is also intended for use in Bible study groups, Sunday School classes, workshops, and high school and college classes. Discussion questions are at the end of each chapter.

At Holden Village the mine tailings are now covered with a layer of gravel, and planting is next. Change is possible. Knowing the importance of the natural world to the Christian walk gives an added dimension to the great commission: *"Go into all the world and proclaim the good news to the whole creation"* (Mark 16:15).

—*Janice E. and Donald R. Kirk*
*Palo Cedro, California*

# Introduction

CHERISH THE EARTH is for all Christians who want support for earth ministry; who want to identify the unique perspective they bring to earth stewardship; who want to know where and how to begin taking care of the earth. The book is also for pastors and teachers who need ready references of creation theme Scripture passages that relate to Christian teaching; for camp and retreat leaders who need creation theme Scriptures for Bible study and campfire programs. Welcome as well are non-Christian readers who want to understand the basic precepts of the Christian faith.

## The Natural World

The Bible contains much Scripture that mentions the natural world. In the beginning God introduces the natural world, and at the same time the Creation of that world introduces the Creator God.

In Part 1 of this book we describe the dynamic earth system, which is marvelous in function and awesome in scope. The research and study that unfolds daily has given us a broad view of the world as a whole and an appreciation of its magnificent design. Through this design, we can sense the hand of the Creator. This revelation gives us a common bond with the early Hebrews who, without benefit of modern scientific analysis, sensed and named the Being behind nature.

## Scripture Search

With the Creation story as a foundation, the natural world provides meaning and vocabulary for the biblical writers. God's creation is the home of the people, the inspiration of the psalmist, the language of love in the Song of Songs, and the imagery of the prophets. The natural world is included in the blessings of the Promised Land. The environment shapes the parables of Jesus. And in Revelation all creatures participate in the joyful praise at the throne of the Lamb.

In Part 2, Scripture passages are gathered to show the importance of the natural world to God and to God's people. The knowledge of the natural world, woven into the Bible in descriptive phrases, metaphors, and a myriad of spiritual truths, shows how our understanding of Christianity is inseparably linked to the environment. Through this imagery the natural world is confirmed as a means whereby humans can discover the Creator, as God works out divine purpose in the history of humankind.

## Earth Stewardship

Because references to the natural world are found throughout the Bible, it is evident that God's creation permeated the culture and thinking of the biblical peoples. They lived closer to the land than we do. But for modern urban societies, the natural world still provides a dwelling place, life-support, and vocation. The natural world also serves as teacher, model, and inspiration.

Yet we are neglecting the environment that is so important to humans, and fouling life-support systems. Few Scriptures deal directly with the environmental issues we presently face. There is no passage that says: "Go forth and save the earth." It is not that simple. The earth, to the writers of the Bible, was not lost. The people were lost, not the earth. *People* needed to be saved, and God made provision for this with the coming of Christ.

In the meantime, what has happened to our home, the earth? Where are we going with our planet? The urgent question of earth stewardship cannot be ignored as we face the daily destruction of habitat, clean water, clean air, and usable land. The natural beauty of the earth is spoiled by the assault of too many people, wasteful lifestyles, human games of greed and power, the devastation of war, and the ignorance of well-meaning persons about the ways of the natural world.

The warning signals of environmental distress have triggered action on the part of caring individuals. The environmental movement has brought together people of varied philosophies to recycle, save animals, and clean beaches. Where does the Christian fit in? What does Christianity offer that is different? What role should Christians take in earth stewardship?

The answers lie in the foundations of the Christian faith. God was first revealed to humans through the natural world. This primary understanding gives Christians a particular stake in the continuing existence of the earth and its creatures. In addition, the first thing God said to Adam and Eve was essentially, "Here is the earth. Take

care of it." This is a serious charge that has not been withdrawn.

Part 3 addresses the present concerns for the natural
environment and the role Christians play in earth stewardship. Because of the nature of Christianity, a way of life
based on love, Christians have something unique to offer
the environment. The outreach of faith unquestionably includes a ministry to a suffering earth, a ministry of caring,
joy, and praise.

# PART 1

# The Natural World

# 1. The Creation Is Good

POISED and spinning in the dark curve of space, the earth moves ever forward on its established orbit. In precise balance, it traces out a contained existence that is orderly in design, functional, and diverse. Yet despite their diversity, the many forms and systems display relationships of great harmony, a harmony that extends throughout the universe and indicates an all-abiding unity.

Wreathed in clouds, resplendent with sapphire blue oceans and a mantle of green, the planet holds the miracle of life. An abundance of plants and animals exists upon the surface of the earth in a rich array of habitats and communities. From rain forest to savannah, from desert to mountains, the biomass represents a lavish outpouring of creativity that flooded the earth, an outpouring that hints of a boundless and inexhaustible love.

"But ask the animals, and they will teach you,
   the birds of the air, and they will tell you;
ask the plants of the earth, and they will teach you,
   and the fish of the sea will declare to you.
Who among all these does not know
   that the hand of the Lord has done this?
In his hand is the life of every living thing
   and the breath of every human being."

                *(Job 12:7-10, NRSV)*

Job is clearly saying that we should turn to the natural world to study its secrets and experience its truth. This is our way of asking the animals and speaking to the earth. Our study is rewarded as we learn of the intricate relationships that connect each part of the universe to every other part. We find structural and functional patterns in the tiniest atom that are similar to or related in some way to the forms in the farthest reaches of the galaxy. We observe behaviors in forms and systems that occur so regularly that they become natural laws—not just of single occurrences, but laws of the universe.

The universe is so extraordinary that it is inconceivable, for those with faith, to think it could have happened by chance. Although we have only a dim understanding of the workings of the universe, a masterful plan may be perceived in the design of natural systems. The harmony observed in the details interwoven in the complex fabric of life bespeak a remarkable caring of the greatest magnitude. The very order of the whole creation indicates a planned and purposeful endeavor. Surely the creation is the work of a Master Craftsman.

Do you not know?
   Have you not heard?
The Lord is the everlasting God,
   the Creator of the ends of the earth. *(Isa. 40:28a)*

God's work as Creator is emphasized throughout Isaiah. In poetry rich and varied, Isaiah affirms the God of Creation. By marshalling divine forces and initiating the processes, God created the universe and the world in which we live. The Lord developed systems and shaped the elements into the forms and patterns of life.

The Genesis stories of the Creation are familiar to all Christians. The details of the creative act are not clear, but we know that initially God spoke and the Creation began (Ps. 33:9; 148:5). Because God spoke, there is a unity in the origin as well as a unity in the design that governs and coordinates the creation.[1] And also because God spoke, we know the origin of the universe is God-centered, not human-centered.

The God-centered creation exists in beauty, a work of goodness and wonder. The sight of stars that beckon from the infinite darkness of a summer night, or a glimpse of the vast sweep of the sea, expands the heart and lifts the spirit. Yet the awesome universe is trivial when compared to the greatness and majesty, the unparalleled power of the Creator, the Master of the universe, who said,

"Turn to me and be saved,
all you ends of the earth;
for I am God, and there is no other." *(Isa. 45:22)*

This wonderful truth is emphasized by Isaiah again and again. He declared the existence of a righteous God, one who saves, and one able to meet our great need and the needs of the earth.

God created the world as a dynamic system never at rest but constantly in motion, coordinating one action with another, seeking the right balance. That balance is a delicate adjustment of all the participating elements reconciled in the whole to bring about sustained existence. The balance helps achieve the harmony that keeps the system going.

For the earth's environments this translates into a give-and-take among the plants and animals that make up a specific ecosystem (the home for a particular mix of living organisms). The microscopic life forms that exist in a drop of water display abilities that work toward this kind of steady maintenance of their habitat. The same abilities are seen everywhere, from mud puddles, to rotten logs, to a saltwater marsh, to the vast plant and animal communities that spread over the land.

These life forms are affected by the fluctuations of the weather, solar, water, earth, and atmospheric processes established as ongoing support systems for life. Natural processes renew and replenish resources.

Everything in an ecosystem has a function. Everything contributes to the whole. The system is so well developed that there is no true waste. All forms are made up of materials that can be recycled back into the environment.

The established order provides for the diversity of life forms, both plant and animal. From the grass on a wind-swept dune to the mossy forest floor, plants are *the* basic food supply of the planet, manufacturing food through the process of photosynthesis. Plants are vital in holding water in the soil and recycling water into the atmosphere and are a major contributor to rainmaking.

Because of their use of carbon dioxide, plants are important in maintaining the oxygen-carbon dioxide balance, thereby helping reduce the greenhouse effect (the warming of the earth's surface caused when greenhouse gases such as carbon dioxide retain heat in the atmosphere). In addition, plants provide the ground cover and shrubbery that holds the soil and shapes habitat for animals. Without plants the earth would literally blow away.

God's creatures play their roles in habitats around the

globe. Each insect, mammal, bird, or other living being is an integral part of the dynamic system. Those that do not fit or do not adapt to the environment vanish, as the system works toward equilibrium. Those that do succeed live in the varied plant communities contribute to the process of respiration, providing much of the carbon dioxide needed by plants for photosynthesis. Living organisms also add nutrients to the soil through waste and decomposition, thereby aiding the growth of plants.

Thus do plants and animals weave a fabric of existence, shifting roles of dominance and supportiveness to find the balance that works. In this way, life sustains life.

When investigating the mysteries of life or probing the secrets of the physical world, many a scientist has been moved to take a leap of faith or been affirmed in an already deep commitment to the Creator God.[2] The grand design; the extraordinary creativity; the ingenious structures; the logical function of a place and purpose for everything; the awesome complexity of the connections; the simplicity of the principles that govern the operating systems; and above all, the overwhelming beauty that stuns trained as well as untrained observers—these all convey a sense of the infinite, a sense of something beyond, a unity that must have come from a Creator God.

The Creator God is sovereign. The Creator God rules the earth in all its abundance. God's rule promotes and blesses life on earth.

So God created the great creatures of the sea and every living and moving thing with which the water teems, according to their kinds, and every winged bird according to its kind. And God saw that it was good. God blessed them and said, "Be fruitful and increase in number and fill the water in the seas, and let the birds increase on the earth." *(Gen. 1:21-22)*

All life is included in this divine blessing, and it is apparent that an abundant and vigorous plant population that supports animals is part of God's plan. We do a blessed work, a godly work, when we appreciate and care for the living plants and animals of the Lord's creation.

We do well to remember that when God finished his creation, the world was a work of art, crafted with care, and beautiful to look upon. God was pleased with it and called it good.

God saw all that he had made, and it was very good.

*(Gen. 1:31a)*

Christians hold that truth within them as they spend their days in the natural world. That truth is a divine viewpoint, a focus for Christian action, Christian use, and Christian care of God's creation.

## Questions for Discussion

1. Why does Job tell us to "ask the animals . . . and birds of the air . . . ask the plants of the earth . . . and the fish of the sea"? How do we ask the animals?

2. What brings unity to the creation?

3. As far as ecosystems are concerned, what are the most important organisms on earth?

4. What enables us to sense the Creator behind the creation?

5. What was God's reaction to the finished creation and forms of life?

# 2. The Condition of the Creation Is Not Good

GOD called the creation good, yet humans do not demonstrate that truth in their dealings with the natural world. Much of the earth is abused and in need of help. The evidence of humanity's misuse litters our land and chokes our waterways. The skies are colored with smog, and the seas are awash with garbage. Even outer space is being littered—not with the stuff of angels but with failed satellites and cast-off space gear.

Humans are not the only abusers of the planet. Prairie dogs normally overpopulate, overgraze, and pollute their villages until about every ten years they have to move. This is not because humans have killed off their predators. They have always been this way. Deer will naturally overbrowse an area until they have to move on. Flocks of certain bird species eat everything in sight. Luckily for them, they can usually fly away from their problem. The crown of thorns starfish, completely apart from any activity of humans, will occasionally destroy thousands of square miles of coral reef and itself in the bargain.

While it is true that other creatures may exploit their habitat, no creature does this quite on the scale of humans. The alarming fact is that humans destroy on a worldwide basis. When the whole earth is not hospitable to life, life cannot continue. We must be alert to the problems and heed the danger signals.

The early warning of any interrupted cycle demands our attention, for it signals an interruption of the patterns of life. Our God is a God of order, and that order permeates the creation.

Even the stork in the sky knows her appointed seasons, and the dove, the swift and the thrush observe the time of their migration. *(Jer. 8:7)*

Jeremiah recognized the orderly pattern of bird migration. In response to the seasonal quality of light and other factors, birds gather and move in flocks to more hospitable climates. The birds fly great distances, navigating by landmarks during the day and by star location at night. Rarely does migration fail to occur, but when this happens it shows that something is wrong with the environment.

The concept of an orderly creation is part of the biblical writings. In the following passage God is declaring that he will maintain a remnant of faithful people until the creation is no more. The creation is described as having "fixed order."

Thus says the Lord,
Who gives the sun for light by day,

And the fixed order of the moon and the stars for light
   by night,
Who stirs up the sea so that its waves roar;
The Lord of hosts is His name:
"If this fixed order departs
From before Me," declares the Lord,
"Then the offspring of Israel also shall cease
From being a nation before Me forever."

                           *(Jer. 31:35-36, NASB)*

The Creator God established orderly patterns in environmental support systems, such as weather, seasons, and tides. God established cycles of life in varied habitats and plant communities. We interfere with those patterns and cycles at our peril.

The early warnings of environmental problems are sounding throughout the earth. As Christians face the global disasters that threaten life on this planet, it is unsettling to find Bible passages such as these:

But your wrongdoing has upset nature's order,
and your sins have kept from you her kindly gifts.

                                *(Jer. 5:25, NEB)*

God makes a home for the lonely;
He leads out the prisoners into prosperity,
Only the rebellious dwell in a parched land.

                                *(Ps. 68:6, NASB)*

Jeremiah is speaking of the autumn and spring rains being withheld by God because of Judah's disobedience. The psalmist touches on the same sort of disharmony. Christians who value the outdoors will be moved to question whether present-day problems are connected to human rebellion and disobedience. The good things that

God has provided need divine controls. Without God, in our care alone, we are finding that the good things God gave us can turn bad.[1]

What wrongdoing has upset nature's order? Will the world's deserts and wastelands increase until there is nowhere else to live? How do we arrive at a theology for earth stewardship? What is the Christian viewpoint on taking care of the earth?

These questions strike at the heart of every Christian who has walked a mountain trail, absorbed the grandeur of a wilderness canyon, relaxed in warm, clear ocean waters, or pondered the veins of a frost-trimmed autumn leaf. The most careful outdoors-person cannot walk through a virgin forest or meadow without leaving a track of some kind. Every human act or movement changes or in some way affects the natural world. This fact multiplied by the number of humans living on the earth underscores the problem. Yet even though humans are numerous, and our lifestyles invasive, Isaiah reminds us that it is God's intent that the world be inhabited.

> For this is what the Lord says—
> he who created the heavens, he is God;
> he who fashioned and made the earth,
>     he founded it;
> he did not create it to be empty,
>     but formed it to be inhabited. *(Isa. 45:18)*

Therefore, it is time to take stock, to seek a Christian perspective for a suffering earth. Plants and animals, blessed by God, are diminishing in kind and number. People around the globe are facing starvation and poor living conditions.

God values the earth for divine purposes. The value of earth to humanity is obvious. The human population of more than 5 billion people cannot live anywhere else. The earth is home.

## Questions for Discussion

1. Who abuses the earth? Why is human abuse such a threat?

2. How do we tell when earth systems are failing?

3. What makes us think our God is a God of order and harmony?

4. What makes humans abuse the earth? Is there a spiritual reason?

5. What was God's intention for the earth? What are God's purposes?

6. How much attention do you pay to the natural world? Do you think most Christians pay too much or too little attention? Why?

# PART 2

## Scripture Search

# 3. The Natural World and God

GOD first revealed himself to the people of earth through the natural world. Early people recognized a supreme will in the natural world that supported them. They named it *El.* This name was not associated with any natural object or phenomenon, but instead described God as the power behind the natural world.

The oldest name by which God was known, *El,* suggests power and authority. God later revealed himself to Israel as *Yahweh* or *Jehovah.* This is variously translated as "He which is" or "He who is truly present." The giving of this name was important, for it unveiled God's nature. Successive names used in Scripture further describe God's nature—Lord of lords, light giver, Father, Judge, Redeemer, Savior, Deliverer, shield, strength, righteous one, and Lord of hosts.

In the Bible we are introduced first to the Creator of the

universe. In succeeding Scriptures God is shown to be infinite, yet personal; concerned with the ongoing function of the created universe, yet interested in the affairs of people.

Many passages tell specifically about the natural world; other passages speak of the creation in metaphor. Whether the natural world is mentioned directly or used as a literary device, it is the creation that gives meaning to the message.

## Natural World Created by God

The great Creation theme of the Bible declares the natural world to be the handiwork of God. Many passages tell that the Lord is the Creator.

> In the beginning God created the heavens and the
> earth.                                          *(Gen. 1:1)*

> "My own hand laid the foundations of the earth,
> and my right hand spread out the heavens."
> *(Isa. 48:13a)*

> You founded the world and all that is in it.   *(Ps. 89:11b)*

Ancient Hebrew thought consistently identified God as the one source of existence. To God as sole Creator belonged the responsibility for the world of nature, including humans. The Lord made all things (Isa. 44:24), and his handiwork is absolutely dependent on him for its ordering and survival.[1]

## Study of the Natural World Reveals God

Scripture says that the natural world is to be studied. Through that study we gain insight, understanding, and knowledge of how things work in nature. We recognize the hand of the Maker in the design and order that prevail.

> I will open rivers on the bare heights,
> And springs in the midst of the valleys;
> I will make the wilderness a pool of water,
> And the dry land fountains of water.
> I will put the cedar in the wilderness,
> The acacia, and the myrtle, and the olive tree;
> I will place the juniper in the desert,
> Together with the box tree and the cypress,
> That they may see and recognize,
> And consider and gain insight as well,
> That the hand of the Lord has done this,
> And the Holy One of Israel has created it.
>
> *(Isa. 41:18-20, NASB)*

To "consider and gain insight" into the natural world is the goal of every scientist. Such study reveals the Creator God.

The wisdom of Solomon included study of the natural world. People came from distant lands to hear his knowledge and seek his counsel.

> God gave Solomon wisdom and very great insight, and a breadth of understanding as measureless as the sand on the seashore. . . . He spoke three thousand proverbs and his songs numbered a thousand and five. He described plant life, from the cedar of Lebanon to the hyssop that grows out of walls. He also taught about animals and birds, reptiles and fish.
>
> *(1 Kings 4:29, 32-33)*

The wisdom literature of the Bible (such as certain Psalms, Proverbs, Job, James) is rich with natural imagery.

The truths in these writings are based on firsthand observation of the natural world and on practical experience. Observing the creation and learning from it constitutes what an educator would call the "perceptual level" of learning. All learning starts at this concrete level of naming and experiencing what is perceived. If it is skipped for some reason, conceptual knowledge may be inaccurate or distorted; theories may not fit actual operation.

Though limited in scope, wisdom literature offered valid direction and help for early peoples. It was also through practical experience with the natural world, that the ancient Hebrews first came to realize the divine force behind nature's ways. Even today it is through the natural world that we come to understand something of the Creator of the universe. This is a concept simple enough for children, and yet holds great depth of meaning for adults.

> Ever since the creation of the world his eternal power and divine nature, invisible though they are, have been understood and seen through the things he has made. So they are without excuse. *(Rom. 1:20, NRSV)*

There are other benefits of nature study. We discover patterns showing us how best to live upon the earth. Applying nature's ways to solve problems is true stewardship. Nature has been the inspiration for many an invention and demonstrates good principles for designing needed processes and products.

Those principles govern the completeness of the design—the impact of resources and energy needed; the destiny of side products and waste products; the final outcome of obsolete or worn-out products. The engineering is not complete unless the true beginning and end of a product are identified and evaluated. In natural systems everything contributes to the maintenance of the natural world. This should be true of everything humans make or produce.

## The Creator God Is Infinite

God created the universe, all things. The one great Creator who could envision such a massive project must, by logic, be greater than the creation that humans perceive.

"It was hidden for long ages in God the Creator of the universe. . . ." *(Eph. 3:10, NEB)*

Can you fathom the mysteries of God?
  Can you probe the limits of the Almighty?
They are higher than the heavens—what can you do?
  They are deeper than the depths of the grave—what can you know?
Their measure is longer than the earth and wider than the sea. *(Job 11:7-9)*

Measured by the limits of the universe, we gain some understanding of the magnitude of the Creator God. Our God is infinite.

## The Creator God Is Personal

Many scriptural passages declare God's love and interest in people, as well as the rest of creation.

Lift up your eyes and look to the heavens:
  Who created all these?
He who brings out the starry host one by one,
  and calls them each by name.
Because of his great power and mighty strength,
  not one of them is missing. *(Isa. 40:26)*

Are not two sparrows sold for a penny? Yet not one of
them will fall to the ground apart from the will of your
Father. And even the very hairs of your head are all
numbered. *(Matt. 10:29-30)*

Part of the mystery of God is that God is infinite and at
the same time personal. Every detail of the whole creation
comes under God's watchful eye. The Almighty is not a
great magician in the sky, but a personal God who cares
for each person and for all the creation.

[God did this] so that they would search for God and
perhaps grope for him and find HIM—though indeed
he is not far from each one of us. For 'In him we live
and move and have our being. . . .
                                    *(Acts 17:27-28a, NRSV)*

God is not far from each one of us, as the author of Acts
knew from personal experience. That experience is available to all, for we are told that we only need to ask (Matt.
7:7-8).

## The Natural World Describes God

Scripture tells us that no one can see God and live (Exod.
33:20). Those who "saw" God saw him in a form used tem-
porarily for the particular occasion. God appeared to Moses in a burning bush, to the Israelites as a pillar of fire by
night, and a cloud by day (Exod. 13:21). Before God called
for Moses to hear the Ten Commandments (Exod. 19:18),
God descended to the top of Mount Sinai in smoke and
fire.
    Natural imagery is used in the Psalms to describe the
attributes of God.

The voice of the Lord is over the waters;
  the God of glory thunders,
  the Lord thunders over the mighty waters.
The voice of the Lord is powerful;
  the voice of the Lord is majestic.
The voice of the Lord breaks the cedars;
  the Lord breaks in pieces the cedars of Lebanon . . .
The voice of the Lord strikes with flashes of lightning.
The voice of the Lord shakes the desert . . .
The voice of the Lord twists the oaks
  and strips the forests bare.
And in his temple all cry, "Glory!" *(Ps. 29:3-9)*

Because we have heard thundering waters and winds, we gain some understanding of what the awesome Creator can be like.

## The Natural World Reveals God's Character

The character of God is shown through the imagery of the created world. God's faithfulness, righteousness, knowledge, power, creativeness, holiness, loving-kindness, justice, and mercy are referred to in many Scriptures that use images from nature.

The heavens praise your wonders, O Lord,
  your faithfulness too. *(Ps. 89:5)*

Love and faithfulness meet together;
  righteousness and peace kiss each other.
Faithfulness springs forth from the earth,
  and righteousness looks down from heaven.
The Lord will indeed give what is good,
  and our land will yield its harvest.
Righteousness goes before him

and prepares the way for his steps. *(Ps. 85:10-13)*

Your love, O Lord, reaches to the heavens,
    your faithfulness to the skies.
Your righteousness is like the mighty mountains,
    your justice like the great deep. *(Ps. 36:5-6)*

The Lord is righteous in all his ways
    and loving toward all he has made. *(Ps. 145:17)*

We can relate to the writings of the psalmists because
we are familiar with the natural world. We can imagine a
love so great that it reaches to the heavens. We can grasp
righteousness so strong and true that it is like mighty
mountains, justice so all-encompassing it is "like the great
deep." And we are told the Lord is "loving toward all he
has made," a statement that includes an awesome number
of living creatures around the globe.

## The Natural World Reveals God's Glory

The psalmist used the theme of the visible creation to sing
of the glory of its Maker.

O Lord my God, you are very great;
    you are clothed with splendor and majesty.
He wraps himself in light as with a garment;
    he stretches out the heavens like a tent
    and lays the beams of his upper chambers on their
        waters.
He makes the clouds his chariot
    and rides on the wings of the wind.
He makes winds his messengers,
    flames of fire his servants. *(Ps. 104:1-4)*

Awed by God's majestic holiness and humbled by God's moral attributes, humans ascribe glory to the Creator. That glory is described in poetic and artistic natural images by the psalmist. In other Bible passages as well, the glory of God is illustrated through manifestations in the physical world.

## God Causes the Natural World to Function

The Scriptures declare that God provides for the very function of the natural world. The essential needs of food, water, and shelter are supplied. This is poetically stated by the psalmist in Psalm 104, the Creation Psalm.

> You make springs gush forth in
>      the valleys;
>    they flow between the hills,
> giving drink to every wild
>      animal;
>    the wild asses quench their
>      thirst
> By the streams the birds of the
>      air have their habitation;
>    they sing among the branches.
> From your lofty abode you water
>      the mountains;
>    the earth is satisfied with the
>      fruit of your work.
>
> You cause the grass to grow for
>      the cattle,
>    and plants for people to use,
> to bring forth food from the
>      earth.

and wine to gladden the
human heart,
oil to make the face shine,
and bread to strengthen the
human heart.
The trees of the Lord are
watered abundantly,
the cedars of Lebanon that he
planted. . . .

Yonder is the sea, great and
wide,
creeping things innumerable
are there.
living things both small and
great.
There go the ships,
and leviathan that you
formed to sport in it.

These all look to you
to give them their food in due
season;
when you give to them, they
gather it up;
when you open your hand.
they are filled with good
things. *(Ps. 104:10-16, 25-28, NRSV)*

The psalmist affirms that the natural world is dependent on God for its order and its continuing existence.

## The Natural World Draws Us Closer to God

Study of the natural world can draw us closer to God, a labor of love for scientists, gardeners, and naturalists. Every

person who seeks respite from daily life may turn to the beauty and inspiration of the natural world. It is common for artists and creative people to go to the outdoors for renewal and inspiration.

> I lift up my eyes to the hills—
> where does my help come from?
> My help comes from the Lord,
> the Maker of heaven and earth. *(Ps. 121:1-2)*

It seems instinctive for every human to want to return to nature. We go to the mountains, the seashore, the great parks, and natural waysides for re-creation. We go to experience the power, the grandeur, and the peace and order of the natural world. We play hard and work hard in the great outdoors, and we rest.

Away from the rush of business, the burden of schedules, the press of family life, we relax into the harmony of God's world and begin to feel that we are an essential part of it. Somehow the seashore becomes an extension of ourselves, the tide a moving rhythm within us. The forest may become our personal sanctuary, the sighing of the wind echoing the sighs of our souls. That sense of belonging runs deep, an undercurrent of community that links us with the Creator.

This sense of belonging is not the same as pantheism. Pantheism is a doctrine which states that all laws, forces, or manifestations of the self-existing universe are God. To the pantheist all things in creation are equal, everything is divine. According to Francis Schaeffer, "The term 'God's creation' has no real place in pantheistic thinking. One simply does not have a *creation*, but only an extension of God's essence."[2]

This is foreign to Christian beliefs. We perceive God as a personality, a being who created the natural world in its goodness and order. The marvelous works of the creation are not of themselves imbued with holiness or sacredness.

It must be obvious even to the casual observer that humanity is different from other animals, yet we are still part of the community of God's creation. This is the community we relate to when enjoying the natural world. The plants and animals have their own integrity. We respect them as the handiwork of God and realize their place and purpose is part of God's plan.

## We Worship the Creator, Not the Creation

Our instincts cause us to return to the outdoors. Surely this is an unconscious yearning, not only for the order and harmony of the natural world, but also for the Creator responsible—the one and only God.

God is spirit (John 4:24); the creation is a material reality. We can see it, touch it, feel it, whereas we cannot directly touch God. We sometimes fall into the trap of worshiping the creation when it is only an expression of the Creator. This was true of many primitive religions in which the people worshiped forms of nature, but the ancient Israelites were warned against this kind of worship.

> You saw no form of any kind the day the Lord spoke to you at Horeb out of the fire. Therefore watch yourselves very carefully, so that you do not become corrupt and make for yourselves an idol, an image of any shape, whether formed like a man or a woman, or like any animal on earth or any bird that flies in the air. . . . And when you look up to the sky and see the sun, the moon and the stars—all the heavenly array—do not be enticed into bowing down to them and worshiping things the Lord your God has apportioned to all the nations under heaven.  *(Deut. 4:15-19)*

They exchanged the truth of God for a lie, and worshiped and served created things, rather than the Creator—who is forever praised. Amen. *(Rom. 1:25)*

Christians appreciate the beauty and complex function of the natural world, but the Lord God Almighty is the focus of our praise and worship.

## The Creator God Is a Loving Ruler

God's rule is firm and purposeful, but Scriptures assure us that God is a loving God. That love extends to the creation.

The earth is full of his unfailing love. *(Ps. 33:5b)*

As we have seen in Psalm 104 and other passages, the earth is under God's watchful care.

Nothing in all creation is hidden from God's sight. . .
*(Heb. 4:13)*

The concept of a loving, personal God is contrary to deism. Deism is the theological doctrine that God created the world and its natural laws but takes no further part in its functioning. The Christian viewpoint refutes this doctrine. Christians believe that God can and does step in, taking a hand in the affairs of the universe whenever he so wills. As Christians we can call upon God through prayer and petition when we need guidance or help, as we work to accomplish God's purpose.

The problem is that although God is a loving God, the creation—nature—is not always benevolent. Natural processes and systems are thoughtless and uncaring. They can be likened to the machinery in a factory, which runs automatically, certainly without personal concern for the business at hand. However, the owner of the factory does care about the business, the product, and the workers. When necessary, the owner intervenes to solve problems or give assistance, particularly when asked. There is purpose in the product. The owner expects the employees to do the work, contribute to that purpose, and care about the product.

In the same way, God cares about the earth, God's created masterwork, and expects us to do the work of tilling and keeping the creation. Because of the beauty and goodness of the creation, we can go about this task with great joy. We reap the benefit of the harvest and find fulfillment in the work.

The natural world is the arena God chose to develop life for a divine purpose. In this arena a three-way arrangement connects God, humans, and the creation. God created and oversees the earth and its inhabitants. The creation reveals God and supports life on earth. Humans reach out to God as we live in the creation. The participants are inseparably linked. If we turn away from God or tamper with our connections with the creation, we suffer from a godless life, and the creation suffers with us.

## Questions for Discussion

1. How was God first revealed to the earth's people? What name for God was given by the early people? What is the significance of that name?

2. Why should we study the natural world?

3. Why is the natural world important in the wisdom literature of the Bible? How does this relate to the way early peoples understood truths?

4. Name ways the imagery of nature is used to describe God and portray the attributes of God.

5. What is the Christian viewpoint on feeling at one with the universe? How does this differ from pantheism?

6. What is deism? What is the Christian viewpoint concerning deism? Does God control the universe or not?

7. What role do the people of God play in the welfare of the environment? Are there benefits?

8. How may a study of the natural world bring us closer to God?

# 4. The Natural World and the Holy Spirit

In the Old Testament the Holy Spirit is viewed as part of God, the divine nature that is vital energy. The Holy Spirit played a part in the creation of the world, bringing order out of chaos and form to matter. Since the Creation, the same Spirit conserves, renews, and withdraws life, performing a vital function in the realm of the natural world.

In the New Testament the Spirit's saving work is carried on, as the Spirit is revealed as one of three persons in the Godhead. The role of the Spirit can be seen in the names by which the Spirit is known—Helper, Guide, Comforter, Protector, Teacher, Indweller, Convictor of Holy Things, Uniter. The Spirit is the spreader of love and prays for us when our own words fail. The Spirit is also the giver of spiritual gifts, which contribute to the establishment and maintenance of the body of Christ.

The Spirit is closely associated with the Word of God, the Holy Scriptures. Peter records that "men moved by the Holy Spirit spoke from God" (2 Pet. 1:21, NASB). According to Timothy, "all Scripture is God-breathed," (2 Tim. 3:16). Thus the Holy Spirit was vital in producing the Bible, the second means through which God revealed himself to humans.

## The Holy Spirit Was Present at the Creation

The world lay waiting as the Spirit of God hovered over it in awesome power and mystery. The Spirit, the Helper, the bearer of grace and glory, was active in the Creation of the world and remains active today.

> Now the earth was formless and empty, darkness was over the surface of the deep, and the Spirit of God was hovering over the waters. *(Gen. 1:2)*

God separated the light from the darkness and formed the sky. The atmosphere blankets the planet, protecting the surface from the extremes of space and distributing the air and water through the patterns of weather.

> By the word of the Lord were the heavens made,
>   their starry host by the breath of his mouth.
> *(Ps. 33:6)*

Oceans were formed, storehouses for the water cycle. These enormous bodies of water modulate the earth's climate, making it habitable.

The dry land appeared, the crust on the earth. This layer of minerals, dirt, and soil is home to living creatures.

## The Holy Spirit Breathed Life into the Creation

The Hebrew word *ruah* is the word for God's Spirit. It is also translated "wind," or "breath," which is the life force of both animals and humans.[1] Scripture tells of the "breath of life."

> Then the Lord God formed the man from the dust of the ground, and breathed into his nostrils the breath of life; and the man became a living being. *(Gen. 2:7, NRSV)*

> This is what God the Lord says—
> he who created the heavens and stretched them out,
>    who spread out the earth and all that comes out of it,
> who gives breath to its people,
>    and life to those who walk on it . . . *(Isa. 42:5)*

> The Spirit of God has made me;
>    the breath of the Almighty gives me life. *(Job 33:4)*

> The God who made the world and everything in it, he who is Lord of heaven and earth, does not live in shrines made by human hands, nor is he served by human hands, as though he needed anything, since he himself gives to all mortals life and breath and all things. *(Acts 17:24-25, NRSV)*

Knowing "the breath of the Almighty gives me life," lends a hallowed quality to the gift of life. Humans undervalue this great gift in its myriad forms; we know of no other living creatures in the universe as yet. The life that bursts forth in habitats and plant communities on this planet, and the human life that oversees it, may be unique.

## The Holy Spirit Renews the Creation

The Holy Spirit that helps and unifies us also connects all life. In addition the Holy Spirit renews us and creation.

> When you send your Spirit,
>     they are created,
>     and you renew the face of the earth. *(Ps. 104:30)*

> He saved us through the washing of rebirth and renewal by the Holy Spirit, whom he poured out on us generously through Jesus Christ our Savior. *(Titus 3:5-6)*

The Holy Spirit energizes us, empowers us, and heals us.[2] Because of the generous outpouring of the Spirit's help as we live the Christian disciplines, we may experience the fruit of the Spirit—joy, peace, long-suffering, gentleness, godliness, faithfulness, meekness and temperance (Gal. 5:22). These fruit of the Spirit are needed in our ministry to the earth and its peoples.

## Justice for the Natural World Follows the Coming of the Spirit

Isaiah foretold the outpouring of the Spirit that was to come with the reign of the Messiah. Abundance in nature is linked with the outpouring of the Spirit. The prophecy also foretells righteousness and justice for the natural world.

> The fortress will be abandoned,
>     the noisy city deserted;
> citadel and watchtower will become a wasteland
>     forever,
>     the delight of donkeys, a pasture for flocks,
> till the Spirit is poured upon us from on high,

and the desert becomes a fertile field,
and the fertile field seems like a forest.
Justice will dwell in the desert
and righteousness live in the fertile field.
The fruit of righteousness will be peace;
the effect of righteousness will be
quietness and confidence forever. *(Isa. 32:14-17)*

Passages such as this have both literal and figurative dimensions. They can be understood literally or spiritually. However, in this particular context, a literal interpretation seems the more appropriate. A judgment has been made, then a blessing comes. The Spirit is "poured upon us," and the result is certainly physical. An intentional sequence is established: prosperity-justice-peace-happiness.

## The Holy Spirit Will Be Within the People; Then the Land Will Become Like the Garden of Eden

Ezekiel envisioned a people with a new heart, a new spirit. He delivered the Word from the Lord, and the prophecy included benefits to the natural world.

A new heart I will give you, and a new spirit I will put within you; and I will remove from your body the heart of stone and give you a heart of flesh. I will put my spirit within you, and make you follow my statutes and be careful to observe my ordinances. Then you shall live in the land that I gave to your ancestors; and you shall be my people, and I will be your God. I will save you from all your uncleannesses, and I will summon the grain and make it abundant and lay no famine upon you. I will make the fruit of the tree and the produce of the field abundant, so that you may never again suffer the disgrace of famine among the nations. . . .

Thus says the Lord God: On the day that I cleanse you from all your iniquities, I will cause the towns to be inhabited, and the waste places shall be rebuilt. The land that was desolate shall be tilled, instead of being the desolation that it was in the sight of all who passed by. And they will say, "This land that was desolate has become like the garden of Eden; and the waste and desolate and ruined towns are now inhabited and fortified." Then the nations that are left all around you shall know that I, the Lord, have rebuilt the ruined places, and replanted that which was desolate; I, the Lord, have spoken, and I will do it.

*(Ezek. 36:26-30, 33-36, NRSV)*

The Spirit of God must first dwell within the people. Then the land will become like the garden of Eden. This promise of restoration begins on earth, and we know it will be fully realized upon the return of our Lord Jesus Christ.

## Questions for Discussion

1. What part did the Holy Spirit play in the Creation? What vital functions in the environment has the Holy Spirit continued to perform?

2. What was the second means through which God was revealed? What did the Holy Spirit have to do with this?

3. What is the "breath of life"?

4. What is the role of the Holy Spirit for Christians? What is the fruit of the Spirit? Why is this important to Christians?

5. Discuss justice for the natural world. Does the Spirit play a part in this justice?

# 5. The Natural World and Jesus Christ

THE Creation started with the Word. The Jews used the term *the Word* to refer to God. The Greeks understood this term to express the ideas of reason and creative control. The Christian understands the Word to refer to Christ.

God has been revealed through the incarnation of Jesus Christ. This is the third means by which God was revealed to humanity. God came to earth in the form of a human being, to live among the people, to be accessible to observation by the human senses (1 John 1:1-3). This same God, however, cannot be comprehended except by the illumination of the Holy Spirit (1 Cor. 2:7-16).

The life of Jesus on earth taught us by word and example how to live the way of the Lord. Through his death and resurrection, Jesus redeemed humans and the whole creation.

Jesus is also called the beloved, Counselor, Deliverer, Emmanuel (God with us), faithful one, head of the church, image of God, King of kings, light of the world, Prince of Peace, Savior and Mediator. He has authority "in heaven and on earth" (Matt. 28:18).

## Christ Was Present at the Creation

In the beginning was the Word, and the Word was with God, and the Word was God. He was with God in the beginning. *(John 1:1-2)*

When God spoke, the earth was created. Humans speculate and argue over just how this was accomplished, for details are not completely known. Yet one thing is assured in the Scriptures—the Word, which we understand to be Christ, was with God at the time of creation.

## All Things Were Made Through Christ

Scripture tells us that all things were made through Christ. The reality of God's creation, extending to the whole universe, was articulated through the Word.

Through him all things were made; without him nothing was made that has been made. *(John 1:3)*

Long ago God spoke to our ancestors in many and various ways by the prophets, but in these last days he has spoken to us by a Son, whom he appointed heir of all things, through whom he also created the worlds.
*(Heb. 1:1-2, NRSV)*

The whole universe has been created through him and for him. *(Col. 1:16, NEB)*

Christ was the instrument of creation, the mediating Agent through whom it actually came into being. The entire life of the universe is mediated from God through Christ.[1]

## In Christ Was Life

God created the mystery we call life, whose many forms sustain and at the same time fascinate us. No one has ever adequately defined life nor duplicated it. Scientists know the ingredients of life but have never discovered its essence. When we contemplate a redwood tree, an amoeba, or even the marvel of the human being, no one can explain what made the collection of chemical compounds come to life. We observe the phenomenon of life, but without God, it makes no sense, holds no purpose, and this will remain true even if science someday duplicates life.

> For with you is the fountain of life;
> in your light we see light. *(Ps. 36:9)*

With the coming of Jesus Christ, God provided the life and light for all humans: salvation and deliverance.

> What has come into being in him was life, and the life was the light of all people. *(John 1:3b-4, NRSV)*

Life on earth is possible because of Christ, through whom all things were made. Life eternal is also possible because of Christ, who became human in the physical world. The life and teaching of Jesus Christ demonstrated the way to eternal life. His life became the light of all people, the hope for all humankind (John 8:12).

## Christ Is Head over All Creation

Paul writes that Christ is the "image of God," "the first-born of all creation." He is also head of the church. Paul emphasizes the supremacy of Jesus Christ.

> He is the image of the invisible God, the firstborn over all creation. For by him all things were created: things in heaven and on earth, visible and invisible, whether thrones or powers or rulers or authorities; all things were created by him and for him. He is before all things, and in him all things hold together.
>
> *(Col. 1:15-17)*

The firstborn son in the Hebrew world had certain rights and privileges. In the same way Christ, being the firstborn Son of God, has certain rights and privileges. That includes sovereignty and preeminence over all the creation. The authors of *Earthkeeping* state that "Scripture teaches a continual, creative, and sustaining presence of God with his creation. And that creative and sustaining presence is understood as the second person of the Trinity, Christ Jesus of Nazareth, who is the Word without which nothing was made."[2]

## Christ Brought Reconciliation to the Natural World

Harmony between God and humans was destroyed when Adam and Eve sinned. At the same time disorder appeared in the creation (Rom. 8:19-22). But since the very beginning God has promised salvation and redemption for humans and restoration of the land.

> For God was pleased to have all his fullness dwell in him, and through him to reconcile to himself all things,

whether things on earth or things in heaven, by making peace through his blood, shed on the cross.

*(Col. 1:19-20)*

When Jesus died, he brought reconciliation to humanity and also to the creation. Peace was now possible between God and all creation. In principle harmony was restored to the physical world, though the full realization of harmony will come only when Christ returns (Rom. 8:21).

## Jesus Used the Natural World for Teaching

Much of Jesus' ministry was outdoors. He walked the roads, climbed the hills, and sat beside the lake, teaching and ministering to the people. He used the natural world to illustrate his parables and teachings.

Likewise every good tree bears good fruit, but a bad tree bears bad fruit. *(Matt. 7:17)*

Therefore everyone who hears these words of mine and puts them into practice is like a wise man who built his house on the rock. The rain came down, the streams rose, and the winds blew and beat against that house.

*(Matt. 7:24-25)*

A farmer went out to sow his seed. As he was scattering the seed, some fell along the path, and the birds came and ate it up. Some fell on rocky places. *(Matt. 13:3-5)*

The kingdom of heaven is like a mustard seed, which a man took and planted in his field. *(Matt. 13:31)*

Once again, the kingdom of heaven is like a net that was let down into the lake and caught all kinds of fish.

*(Matt. 13:47)*

These parables spoke to a society that lived closely with the great outdoors, tending livestock and farming. By using stories from the natural world, Jesus not only used an effective teaching tool, he validated the reality and integrity of the natural world. As Granberg-Michaelson points out in *A Worldly Spirituality*, "The frequent appeals of Christ to the created world in his teaching underscores its trustworthiness, value, and integrity. . . . the creation possesses the qualities from which we can learn the deepest truths of life." [3]

## Jesus Tells How to Approach Earthkeeping

Blessed are the gentle,
for they shall inherit the earth. *(Matt. 5:5, NASB)*

Jesus is repeating the words of Psalm 37:11. Those who humbly acknowledge their dependence on the goodness and grace of God and betray no arrogance toward other people will inherit the land. Other versions of the Bible replace the word "gentle" with "meek" (NIV) or a "gentle spirit" (NEB). In terms of keeping the creation, this is a great contrast to the quarrelsome, aggressive behavior of many of the earth's peoples.

Jesus' words nudge us to the realization that our behavior needs to change, and that the change is not only outward, but also inward. Until the inner attitudes, desires, and motives are refocused, the outward behaviors will be a constant burden to the earth.

The inner change starts when we admit our shortcomings and sins and recognize that we are terribly alone. If we believe Jesus Christ is Lord with power to forgive sins, then we can make the decision to accept his offer of salvation. This is a simple act accomplished by asking Jesus to come into our hearts.

The Christian way is not just an intellectual exercise. It must be experienced. To do that we make Jesus Christ the ruler of our lives. Through prayer we communicate our needs and ask for divine guidance. This results in day-to-day trust and obedience.

We join with other Christians for Bible study, worship, fellowship, and ministry. We begin a new life built on the teachings of Jesus. The love of God that subsequently pours into our lives will trigger the spiritual growth that brings us healing and wholeness. A faith based on the love of God then becomes an outreach of service, to others, and to the entire creation.

## Questions for Discussion

1. What is the third way that God was revealed to humans?

2. What does the *Word* mean to Jews and Christians? What does this have to do with the Creation?

3. Discuss Romans 8:19-22. What are the implications for the natural world?

4. How did Jesus use the natural world in his ministry? What does this tell us about the importance of the environment?

5. What kind of earth caretakers ought we to be? How do we accomplish this?

# 6. The Natural World and Humankind

THE Scriptures tell us that humans were formed from the dust of the earth and became living souls when the Lord God Almighty breathed life into their bodies. "Male and female he created them" (Gen. 1:27, NRSV).

Humans are linked physically with organic nature. We are part of the creation. At the same time humans have a spiritual endowment that allows transcendence of nature. This capacity for spiritual growth and understanding makes it possible for people to recognize God and to distinguish between good and evil. Scripture records how frequently humans fail to measure up to divine standards and expectations. Nevertheless people are born with an ability to respond to God and with a capacity for hope.

## Humans Are Created in the Image of God

Formed in the image of God, humans walk the earth. Because people are made in God's image, every human being is worthy of honor and respect.

> Then God said, "Let us make humankind in our image, according to our likeness, and let them have dominion over the fish of the sea, and over the birds of the air, and over the cattle, and over all the wild animals of the earth, and over every creeping thing that creeps upon the earth.
> So God created humankind in his image,
> in the image of God he created them;
> male and female he created them.
> *(Gen. 1:26-27, NRSV)*

Although God's holy qualities are beyond our comprehension, humans are nevertheless capable of reflecting to some degree the characteristics of God. Righteousness, creativity, knowledge, wisdom, holiness, justice, compassion, and mercy are traits needed by humanity to carry out the work we have been given. When operating on our own strength we do not consistently express these qualities, but we do live them out when empowered by the Holy Spirit.

## God Gave Humans Vocation: Earth Stewardship

The first inhabitants of the earth inherited paradise, but paradise brought responsibility. God blessed humanity with a vocation. We are not meant to be idle. We are the keepers of the garden, delegated sovereigns of the earth.

> The Lord God took the man and put him in the garden of Eden to till it and keep it. *(Gen. 2:15, NRSV)*

You have given them dominion
    over the works of your hands;
    you have put all things under their feet.
all sheep and oxen,
    and also the beasts of the field,
the birds of the air, and the fish
        of the sea,
    whatever passes along the
        paths of the seas. *(Ps. 8:6-8, NRSV)*

Our record as earthkeepers is poor. We have brought the world to the brink of environmental disaster. However, as the church scrambles to establish a Christian earth ministry, there is hope. If we take up the work without delay, laboring with knowledge and diligence, it is possible for the earth to experience extraordinary renewal.

## Humans Are Part of the Natural World

In the great creation psalm, Psalm 104, the psalmist describes the natural world in poetic detail. Surprisingly, human activity rates only four lines. Humanity is treated as just one part of the total picture.

You cause the grass to grow for
        the cattle,
    and plants for people to use.
to bring forth food from the
        earth. . . .

People go out to their work
    and to their labor until the
        evening. *(Ps. 104:14, 23, NRSV)*

Although God has given humans dominion over the natural world, humanity is not separate from the natural world. People are part of each community that inhabits planet Earth. We play a special role in the habitats where we dwell, but we are also part of those habitats. An element of our participation is that we take on the particular responsibility for the welfare of the environment.

Our attitude toward the earth fluctuates wildly. On the one hand we aggressively misuse the earth, wiping out resources and treating plant and animal communities with utter and often cruel disregard.

On the other hand, we romanticize the natural world. We anthropomorphize animals and sometimes plants. This means that we inappropriately attribute human feelings and motivations to them. We sentimentalize the great outdoors until we forget the lessons of biology—that nature is not always benevolent, and an instinct for survival is at the root of much behavior.

Humans hold a special position. We are consciously connected to God and to the Lord's creation. We look upward to our Maker, and outward to the natural world. Our unique role is a humbling one. We serve God by serving his creation, including our fellow human beings.

## Humans Are God's Handiwork

Humankind are different from other animals. What sets humans apart involves such things as an ability for spoken language; a large, complex brain that allows thinking operations like reasoning and reflection; and the ability to detach ourselves from the present to consider past and future. Humans can perceive a spiritual dimension to the universe. We recognize the handiwork of God in the creation, and we sense the love that was poured into the world that was created.

We are God's work of art, created in Christ Jesus to live the good life as from the beginning he had meant us to live it.

*(Eph. 2:10, JB)*

For we are God's workmanship, created in Christ Jesus to do good works, which God prepared in advance for us to do.

*(Eph. 2:10)*

We are the handiwork of God, made in love and created for a purpose. God has prepared work for us to do, work that includes taking care of the earth.

## God Loves His People

Each individual is genetically unique. No person, not even an identical twin, has ever existed, or will appear, who is exactly like another. None of us is perfect, yet we are the product of a God who loves and cares for us.

For you created my inmost being;
　　you knit me together in my mother's womb.
I praise you because I am fearfully and wonderfully made;
　　your works are wonderful,
　　I know that full well.
My frame was not hidden from you
　　when I was made in the secret place.
When I was woven together in the depths of the earth,
　　your eyes saw my unformed body.
All the days ordained for me
　　were written in your book
　　before one of them came to be. *(Ps. 139:13-16)*

When I look at your heavens,
> the work of your fingers,
> the moon and the stars that
> you have established;
what are human beings that you
> are mindful of them,
> mortals that you care for
> them? *(Ps. 8:3-4, NRSV)*

Imperfect, incomplete, we lead our daily lives, assured by Scripture that we are loved. We can recognize God's love, and when we ask, we can receive that love in the very core of our beings.

## Human Sin Affected the Earth

The disobedience of Adam and Eve in the garden of Eden separated them from God. Their disobedience also affected the earth.

To Adam he said, "Because you listened to your wife and ate from the tree about which I commanded you, 'You must not eat of it,'
> "Cursed is the ground because of you;
> > through painful toil you will eat of it
> > all the days of your life.
> It will produce thorns and thistles for you.
> > > > > *(Gen. 3:17-18)*

This disobedience is another creation theme that runs through Scripture. Human obedience to God is somehow linked to the condition of the creation.

## Questions for Discussion

1. What does it mean to be formed "in the image of God"?

2. What is the relationship of humans to the natural world?

3. What is the relationship of humans to God?

4. How do you make sense of a good God and a natural order often rooted in competition for survival?

# 7. The Natural World and Obedience

CHRISTIANS are called by God to obedience. The act of obedience is realized inwardly and outwardly. Internal obedience springs from the inner response and spiritual attitude of the believer. External obedience is acted out as observable behavior. The two do not always agree, but true obedience begins as an inner attitude acted out externally.

Christian obedience is more than an outward response to authority in order to gain reward or avoid punishment. When we perceive the greatness and goodness of the Almighty, we respond. Filled with God's love, we are ready to obey his commands and serve him.

We obey God, first of all, because of who God is. The Lord's very goodness is the basis for obedience (Ps. 145, Acts 14:17). We love God because the Lord is so faithful, trustworthy, and righteous—and because God loves us. In addition, we obey God because of the loving redemption of humankind and all the creation.

We fail to obey God when we ignore the commands and instructions written in the Bible. The failure of humans to obey God's word and follow Jesus' teachings results in an ungodly life. Scripture also relates how our failure to obey affects the welfare of the natural world, bringing ruin and neglect to the creation.

## Obedience in Eden

Throughout the Bible the condition of the creation is linked to the behavior of the people. The trouble started at the very beginning when Adam and Eve disobeyed the Lord's command.

> You are free to eat from any tree in the garden; but you must not eat from the tree of the knowledge of good and evil, for when you eat of it you will surely die.
>
> *(Gen. 2:16-17)*

Adam and Eve failed to obey this command and because of sin fell out of harmony with God. The result of this disobedience was also disharmony with the creation.

> Cursed is the ground because of you. *(Gen. 3:17)*

Paradise was a created world based on harmonious relationships. But the divine plan and purpose for the earth was thwarted when we separated ourselves from God by an act of disobedience. The harmony was broken.

## Obedience in the Promised Land

As God prepared the Israelites for the Promised Land, Moses recorded promise after promise from the Lord. The promised blessings for the people were always linked to the blessings of the land—rain, fruitful harvest, well-being.

> If you follow my decrees and are careful to obey my commands, I will send you rain in its season, and the ground will yield its crops and the trees of the field their fruit. Your threshing will continue until grape harvest and the grape harvest will continue until planting, and you will eat all the food you want and live in safety in your land. *(Lev. 26:3-5)*

In the days of the old covenants, the future of the creation was linked to the obedience of the people.

> If you heed these ordinances, by diligently observing them, the Lord your God will maintain with you the covenant loyalty that he swore. . . . he will love you, bless you. . . . he will bless the fruit of your womb and the fruit of your ground, your grain and your wine and your oil, the increase of your cattle and the issue of your flock. *(Deut. 7:12-13, NRSV)*

> Therefore keep the commandments of the Lord your God, by walking in his ways and by fearing him. For the Lord your God is bringing you into a good land, a land with flowing streams, with springs and underground waters . . . a land of wheat and barley, of vines and fig trees and pomegranates, a land of olive trees and honey, a land where you may eat bread without scarcity . . . a land whose stones are iron and from whose hills you may mine copper. You shall eat

your fill and bless the Lord your God for the good land
that he has given you. *(Deut. 8:6-10, NRSV)*

So if you faithfully obey the commands I am giving you
today—to love the Lord your God and to serve him
with all your heart and with all your soul—then I will
send rain on your land in its season, both autumn and
spring rains, so that you may gather in your grain, new
wine and oil. I will provide grass in the fields for your
cattle, and you will eat and be satisfied. . . .

*(Deut. 11:13-15)*

The promises were repeated again and again, but they
always hinged on the injunction to obey God. Also recorded were curses for disobedience—disease, scorching heat
and drought, blight and mildew, "the sky over head will be
bronze, the ground beneath you iron. The Lord will turn
the rain of your country into dust and powder; it will come
down from the skies until you are destroyed." Oppression,
a small harvest, fearful plagues, harsh and prolonged disasters, and severe and lingering illnesses were among the
results of disobedience (Deut. 28:15-68).

In those ancient times the key to blessing was obedience. Failure to obey God's laws brought devastation, not
only to the people, but to nature.

## Christian Obedience

It would be a mistake to think that God uses blessings and
curses to control behavior through reward and punishment. There is a deeper aspect to obeying the Lord, a spiritual significance. When Saul turned his back on the Lord,
he claimed he had been carrying out the Lord's instruc-
tion. Samuel responded,

> Does the Lord delight in burnt offerings and sacrifices
>    as much as in obeying the voice of the Lord?
> To obey is better than sacrifice,
>    and to heed is better than the fat of rams.
>
> *(1 Sam. 15:22)*

Rebellion cost Saul his throne, just as Moses was barred from the Promised Land due to disobedience (Num. 20:12). Rebellion cost a whole generation of Hebrews their inheritance (Num. 14:26-35) as they wandered in the wilderness awaiting entry into the Promised Land.

Humanity's rebellion has also cost the creation. Our failure is obvious in the glaring devastation of the environment. The crux of the problem lies deep, in our separation from God and our failure to do God's will in taking care of the earth.

The key to blessing is still obedience, but for the Christian the act of obedience is an outward behavior motivated by an inner desire to honor God's love and accept God's Sovereignty. Paul encouraged the Galatians,

> For you reap whatever you sow. If you sow to your own flesh, you will reap corruption from the flesh, but if you sow to the Spirit, you will reap eternal life from the Spirit. So let us not grow weary in doing what is right. *(Gal. 6:7-9, NRSV)*

James also wrote on obedience.

> But be doers of the word, and not merely hearers who deceive themselves. For if any are hearers of the word and not doers, they are like those who look at themselves in a mirror; for they look at themselves and, on going away, immediately forget what they were like. But those who look into the perfect law, the law of

liberty, and persevere, being not hearers who forget
but doers who act—they will be blessed in their doing.
*(James 1:22-25, NRSV)*

Because of who the Lord is and what the Lord asks, we
make a personal decision of trust and commitment, the result of our faith. That trust and commitment are acted out
in living service. This is obedience from an inner compul-
sion, a personal love of God that spills over into doing
God's work.

"My food," said Jesus, "is to do the will of him who sent
me and to finish his work. Do you not say, 'Four
months more and then the harvest'? I tell you, open
your eyes and look at the fields! They are ripe for harvest." *(John 4:34-35)*

The followers of Jesus have special work in tending
fields ripe for harvest—both literally in maintaining God's
creation, and figuratively as they spread the gospel.

## Questions for Discussion

1. What is Christian obedience? How has our obedience or lack of obedience affected the environment?
2. What were the Old Testament promises and curses
and their effect on the land?
3. What is the New Testament message on obedience?
What did Jesus say about obedience?
4. Give examples of times your outward behavior has
been motivated by inner promptings of the Spirit.

# 8. The Natural World and Covenant

Our God is a covenant God. Over the centuries the Almighty has made binding agreements with chosen people. In each agreement, God promised something. Some of the covenants were unconditional, but others hinged on the condition that humans would do something in return. The covenants usually had to do with redemption. God made covenants with Noah, Abraham, the people of Israel, Phinehas, and David before promising a New Covenant. The New Covenant was accomplished through the sacrifice of Jesus Christ.

The ancient covenant with Noah included promises for the natural world. The New Covenant also includes God's creation. It is a covenant of pure grace in which God's law is in our minds and written on our hearts (Jer. 31:33).

## God's Covenant for the Natural World

After Eden, humans continued to live apart from God, growing increasingly disobedient, until God grieved that he had made them and resolved to send a Flood. God's saving hand was extended to one righteous man, Noah, and his family. In the story of the ark, God directed Noah to save the animals and also the food supply—plants.

After the Flood God made a covenant with Noah that included all the creation, promising never again to destroy all living creatures and the earth by the waters of a flood. As a sign, the Lord set the rainbow in the clouds.

> Then God said to Noah and to his sons with him: "I now establish my covenant with you and with your descendants after you and with every living creature that was with you—the birds, the livestock and all the wild animals, all those that came out of the ark with you—every living creature on earth. I establish my covenant with you: Never again will all life be cut off by the waters of a flood; never again will there be a flood to destroy the earth." *(Gen. 9:8-11)*

This covenant is a pledge for all the creation, not just people. In the words of Granberg-Michaelson, "God is with the creation. God's purposes for the creation will endure. What God has made, God will not forsake. Rather, the creation will be renewed and redeemed. It will be won back to God." [1]

A covenant made by God is a promise forever. The covenant is eternal.

> As long as the earth endures,
> seedtime and harvest,
> cold and heat,
> summer and winter,

day and night
will never cease. *(Gen. 8:22)*

This is a sign of the covenant I am making between me
and you and every living creature with you, a covenant
for all generations to come. *(Gen. 9:12)*

Never again will the waters become a flood to destroy
all life. *(Gen. 9:15)*

Whenever the rainbow appears in the clouds, I will see
it and remember the everlasting covenant between
God and all living creatures of every kind on the earth.
*(Gen. 9:16)*

Noah, the receiver of the covenant, was a righteous
man, obedient to the Lord even to the extent of building an
ark on dry ground. But humans have since failed in obedience and trust. We hold the weak side of the bargain. We
can refuse to honor a covenant. We can neglect any agreement with God.

## The Natural World Suffers
## When a Covenant Is Broken

When the Israelites again broke the covenant, the creation
suffered. The link between the broken covenant and the
fate of creation is a recurring biblical theme.

The earth dries up and withers,
   the world languishes and withers,
   the exalted of the earth languish.
The earth is defiled by its people;
   they have disobeyed the laws,
violated the statutes

and broken the everlasting covenant.
Therefore a curse consumes the earth;
  its people must bear their guilt. *(Isa. 24:4-6)*

The people of God ignored divine guidance. Their rebellion cut off any help from God in managing the earth. When that happened, the earth suffered. Scripture reinforces the fact that humans are a major reason for devegetation of the earth. Human activities, including domestic animals allowed to roam uncontrolled in certain areas, have been a prime force in enlarging and sometimes even forming the world's deserts.

How does this happen? Desert plants are normally adapted to hard times, but when they are trampled by people and animals, they can be fatally damaged. Tender new growth, which may be sparse, is destroyed. Then when the inevitable drought times occur, the plants do not have the resistance nor the numbers to survive.

Plant life sustains animal existence and helps to control the climate and shape habitats. We know this, yet the very plant forms that sustain us are being destroyed, a result of our separation from God and our neglect of the environment. We are called to be obedient servants—but disobey.

## New Covenant Includes the Natural World

God is faithful. God never gives up. In due time the ancient prophets revealed God's promise of a new covenant. The new covenant included the natural world.

"In that day I will make a covenant for them
  with the beasts of the field and the birds of the air
  and the creatures that move along the ground.
Bow and sword and battle
  I will abolish from the land,

> so that all may lie down in safety.
> I will betroth you to me forever;
>> I will betroth you in righteousness and justice,
>> in love and compassion.
> I will betroth you in faithfulness,
>> and you will acknowledge the Lord.
> In that day I will respond,"
>> declares the Lord—
> "I will respond to the skies,
>> and they will respond to the earth;
> and the earth will respond to the grain,
>> the new wine and oil,
>> and they will respond to Jezreel.
> I will plant her for myself in the land;
>> I will show my love to the one I
>> called 'Not my loved one.'
> I will say to those called 'Not my people,' 'You are
>> my people';
>> and they will say, 'You are my God.' " *(Hos. 2:18-23)*

When Christ is king, the people will be reconciled to God, and there will be peace. The skies as well as the earth and its products will prosper as righteousness and justice spread.

Through Jesus Christ, humanity and all creation will be redeemed. This is an act of pure grace on the part of the Almighty, sending us an unmerited gift of salvation. The terms of the covenant are simply, "I will take you as my own people, and I will be your God."[2]

Since war is still a fact of life on earth, it is evident that this Scripture has not totally been fulfilled. Yet as God's bearers of the gospel, we can carry the message of peace, extending and supporting God's plan for the human population and the natural world.

## Questions for Discussion

1. What is a covenant? What covenants did God make with Noah, Abraham, the people of Israel, Phinehas, and David?

2. What happened to the environment when the people broke the covenant with God?

3. What is the New Covenant? How does it affect the natural world?

# 9. The Natural World and Justice

RIGHTEOUSNESS flows from God's nature, an outgrowth of divine love. He acts fairly and rightly, and "all his ways are just" (Deut. 32:4). God's will is the standard of equality, the supreme rule of justice.

Justice means that all humans, whether good or bad, will receive their due.[1] Justice certainly includes the act of judgment in assessing right and wrong. But justice is also concerned with right conduct. This definition of justice in the ethical sense became identified with rightly treating the poor through giving alms and other helps.[2] That same conduct we extend to the natural world when we become good stewards of God's creation.

The justice of God is connected with the natural world in many passages. Whether in metaphor or as literal meaning, justice for the natural world is linked to human spiritual life and behavior.

## Our God Is a God of Justice

Passage after passage tells us that our God is a God of justice.

> For the Lord is righteous,
> he loves righteous deeds;
> the upright shall behold his face. *(Ps. 11:7, NRSV)*

> So this is what the Sovereign Lord says:
> "See, I lay a stone in Zion,
>   a tested stone,
> a precious cornerstone for a sure foundation;
>   the one who trusts will never be dismayed.
> I will make justice the measuring line
>   and righteousness the plumb line. *(Isa. 28:16-17)*

> Yet the Lord longs to be gracious to you;
>   he rises to show you compassion.
> For the Lord is a God of justice.
>   Blessed are all who wait for him! *(Isa. 30:18)*

Righteousness, compassion, love, and justice are the characteristics of God. As such, they become the standards for human behavior.

## Justice Extends to the Natural World

The Lord's justice is imparted to all the earth. The whole creation is included in this justice.

The Lord loves righteousness and justice;
the earth is full of his unfailing love. *(Ps. 33:5)*

"But let him who boasts boast about this:
that he understands and knows me,
that I am the Lord, who exercises kindness,
justice, and righteousness on earth,
for in these I delight,"
declares the Lord. *(Jer.9:24, NIV)*

As servants of the living God, we are concerned with the human condition and the condition of the natural world. We are called to extend equality to the oppressed and the poor, to support opportunity for all. We also extend justice to the whole creation.

## God's Judgment Linked to the Natural World

In chapter 25[3] of Jeremiah, the prophet speaks of the many judicial acts of God, concluding with the effect on the creation. God's judgment for humans affected the natural world. Once again we find that when people turn away from God, the creation suffers.

For the Lord is destroying their pasture.
The peaceful meadows will be laid waste
because of the fierce anger of the Lord.
Like a lion he will leave his lair,
and their land will become desolate. *(Jer. 25:36-38)*

The sins of the people cause the Lord to move in anger. The peaceful meadows will suffer. The metaphor of the lion shows the Lord abandoning his own land after it is laid waste.

## Justice for the Oppressed Linked With the Natural World

In contrast to the previous passage, the psalmist links God's justice for oppressed and needy people with an *abundance* in nature. The psalmist stresses the relationship between God and the environment, a vision that unites the liberation of the oppressed with restoring and preserving God's creation.[4]

> Give the king your justice,
>      O God,
>         and your righteousness to a
>         king's son.
> May he judge your people with
>      righteousness,
>         and your poor with justice.
> May the mountains yield
>      prosperity for the people,
>         and the hills, in righteousness.
> May he defend the cause of the
>      poor of the people,
>         give deliverance to the needy,
>         and crush the oppressor. . . .
> May he be like rain that falls on
>      the mown grass,
>         like showers that water the
>         earth.
> In his days may righteousness
>      flourish
>         and peace abound, until the
>         moon is no more. . .
> May there be abundance of
>      grain in the land;
>         may it wave on the tops of the
>         mountains;

> may its fruit be like Lebanon;
> and may people blossom in the
>      cities
> like the grass of the field. *(Ps. 72:1-4, 6-7, 16, NRSV)*

The psalmist succinctly touches on the fact that economic and environmental problems are related—a truth apparent to those who work with underdeveloped countries and oppressed peoples.

To live we develop the land. To develop land, we cut the forests. When the forest is gone, the water runoff increases. The water picks up soil, washing away the topsoil, eroding hillsides and destroying stream banks. The soil is carried downstream, and silt is deposited in rivers and lakes, clogging the waterways. Air pollution and acidification also play a part in killing forests and lakes. When the forests are gone, less moisture transpires into the atmosphere, and the climate is affected.

To develop a product, we gather resources. When the easily accessible resources give out, we dig deeper, stripping off the living habitats and destroying watersheds. When local resources are gone, we turn to other areas or other countries, depleting their stock of resources. To refine, transport, and use these raw materials, we consume fossil fuels and high-cost power. In making products we may produce unnecessary waste. Sometimes that waste is so toxic nothing can live in it or near it. Some of that waste will remain toxic for thousands of years.

Because our problems are linked in a complex system of cause and effect, we know that environmental stresses are connected to patterns of economic development. We see that poor agricultural policies may lie at the root of land, water, and forest destruction. Energy policies are associated with the global greenhouse effect and with deforestation for fuelwood in many developing nations.

The good news is that our debt to the environment can be repaid. With a change of heart and lifestyle, we have a chance of restoring God's creation. Although the problems seem monumental, diverse, and scattered, they really are not separate. Since environmental stresses are linked to one another, our successes in one area, such as forest protection, will improve chances of success in another area, such as soil conservation.[5]

A Christian viewpoint will integrate economics and ecology into decision-making and law-making processes. This will not only protect the environment, but also protect and promote development. Such an approach also supports a new way of life, one following the principles and practices of Christianity. The new way of living must bring lifestyles into better balance with the workings of the creation.

## The Natural World and Shalom

When humans hinder or abolish God's justice throughout the earth, progress fails—the systems fall short for people as well as animals and plants. The broken harmony is not the wholeness intended by God, a wholeness conveyed by the Hebrew term *shalom*. Usually translated as "peace," shalom includes not just an absence of conflict but a concept of total well-being. In its deepest application, shalom means a spiritual peace through restored relations of harmony with God.[6]

Shalom is the result of God's design and rule. It is what God established in the creation from the beginning.

Lord, you establish peace for us;
all that we have accomplished you have done for us.

*(Isa. 26:12)*

Shalom is what God continually seeks to reestablish and renew. Restoring shalom to the earth is not limited to justice among people. Peace and well-being for the earth means shalom for the whole creation.[7]

Justice will dwell in the desert
    and righteousness live in the fertile field.
The fruit of righteousness will be peace;
    the effect of righteousness will be quietness
    and confidence forever. *(Isa. 32:16-17)*

Shalom for the earth is a rich vision that includes the spiritual peace and unity for the creation designed by God. This unity encompasses right relationships as well as a harmony in function and purpose which brings security, well-being, and joy to every creature.

## Justice and Restoration

The restoration of shalom to the earth is repeatedly mentioned in the Old Testament. The separation from God will end, the disharmony among people will be resolved, and the alienation from the creation will be healed. For those who gain "a new heart" and "a new spirit," the restored creation will be "like the garden of Eden" (Ezek. 36:26-35).

The Old Testament writers saw that the Lord would usher in the reign of shalom through the Anointed One, the Christ, the Prince of Peace.[8]

For a child has been born for us,
    a son given to us;
authority rests upon his
    shoulders;
    and he is named

Wonderful Counselor, Mighty
    God,
    Everlasting Father, Prince of
    Peace.
His authority shall grow
    continually,
    and there shall be endless
    peace
for the throne of David and his
    kingdom.
    He will establish and uphold it
with justice and with
    righteousness
    from this time onward and
    forevermore.
The zeal of the Lord of hosts
    will do this. *(Isa. 9:6-7, NRSV)*

The prophet wrote that the promised Messiah would
bring justice and peace not only to humanity, but also to
the creation.

The wolf shall live with the lamb,
    the leopard shall lie down with the kid,
the calf and the lion and the fatling together,
    and a little child shall lead them.
The cow and the bear shall graze,
    their young shall lie down together;
    and the lion shall eat straw like the ox.
The nursing child shall play over the hole of the asp,
    and the weaned child shall put its hand on the
    adder's den.
They will not hurt or destroy on all my holy mountain,
    for the earth will be full of the knowledge of the Lord
    as the waters cover the sea. *(Isa. 11:6-9, NRSV)*

As we reflect upon these apocalyptic writings, we note they do not diminish the diversity of creation, nor speak of it as something to be destroyed. The authors of *Earthkeeping* remark, "How such a noncarnivorous world could in fact be sustained is a mystery to us, but certainly it is no greater than the mystery of the creation itself." [9] And the focus of the Isaiah passage is plainly understood—the richness and complexity of the natural world will be in harmony with humanity, with itself, and with God.

## God's Command: Pursue Justice

"Justice, and only justice, you shall pursue, that you may live and possess the land which the Lord your God is giving you. *(Deut. 16:20, NASB)*

God's command is clear. Also clear is God's example—that of exercising righteousness, kindness, and justice throughout the earth. Our only hope of following God's leading is to start on our knees, with prayer and petition for divine guidance.

Sow for yourselves in justice,
    and you will reap what loyalty deserves.
Break up your fallow;
for it is time to seek the Lord,
seeking him till he comes and gives you just measure
    of rain.
You have ploughed wickedness into your soil,
and the crop is mischief. *(Hos. 10:12-13, NEB)*

How to extend justice to the earth's peoples is an ongoing debate that varies from culture to culture, from region to region. How to recognize, educate, or otherwise support local stewardship of the earth also presents different problems in different areas. "The fact is . . . that literally millions of people around the world have insufficient control over the earth's resources to prevent their own and their children's starvation." The oppressed and poor lack not only the education, but also the opportunity for "stewardship possibilities." [10]

The authors of *Earthkeeping* suggest a "principle of minimal justice" which means that "a nation—or a world—will have a just economic system only if it provides opportunity for all the people to have sufficient income to draw enough from the earth's resources to meet basic needs." [11]

> The Lord looked and was displeased
>   that there was no justice.
> He saw that there was no one,
>   he was appalled that there was no one to
>       intervene. . . .
>
> *(Isa. 59:15b-16)*

In Isaiah's time, the Lord "was appalled that there was no one to intervene," and subsequently stepped in to make things right. Today while politicians and governments move toward a more just world, individuals can exercise justice and stewardship on a personal level. The sum total of many acts of kindness, righteousness, and compassion will bring extraordinary change to the world's oppressed, as well as to the overused and neglected natural world. This is especially true when the acts of kindness are not just righteous deeds, but the outworking of the Holy Spirit.

## Questions for Discussion

1. Define justice. What are the two aspects of justice?
2. Since our God is a God of justice, what does this im-

ply for us as Christians? How far does God's justice extend?

3. What is the relationship between oppressed people and the state of the environment?

4. Discuss the Christian viewpoint that connects ecology and economics.

5. How does the concept of shalom affect the natural world?

6. Think of five ways to pursue justice in your home, your workplace, your community, your country.

7. What would the "principle of minimal justice" mean in your locality?

# 10. The Natural World and Redemption

THE Bible begins with the story of the Creation. The concept of redemption follows that introduction. These two themes are linked again in the Psalms. The redemption theme in Psalm 103 is followed by the story of Creation in Psalm 104. Again in Revelation, the affirmation of the Creation (Rev. 4:11) is followed by affirmation of the redemption (Rev. 5:9-10), and then the praise of every creature in heaven and on earth (Rev. 5:13). The juxtaposition of the two themes throughout the Bible affirms the importance of the natural world. The Creation of the natural world seemingly sets the stage for the concept of redemption.

In addition, there are specific passages dealing with the restoration and redemption for the natural world itself. The important point in the passages is that humans alone will not successfully restore the natural world. The creation is not human-centered, but God-centered. We need God's help. We need to be in harmony with the Creator. We need the filling and guidance of the Holy Spirit.

## The Natural World and Restoration

The Bible records the fluctuating tide of human behavior in falling away from God and coming back. Time after time, God extends love to his people and welcomes their return. The promised blessings include restoration of the land.

> The Lord will surely comfort Zion
> and will look with compassion on all her ruins;
> he will make her deserts like Eden,
> her wastelands like the garden of the Lord.
> Joy and gladness will be found in her,
> thanksgiving and the sound of singing. *(Isa. 51:3)*

> For out of Zion shall go forth
> instruction.
> and the word of the Lord from
> Jerusalem.
> He shall judge between many
> peoples,
> and shall arbitrate between
> strong nations far away;
> they shall beat their swords into
> plowshares,
> and their spears into pruning
> hooks. . . .
> but they shall all sit under their
> own vines and under their
> own fig trees. *(Mic. 4:2b-4, NRSV)*

This famous passage from Micah gives a vision of the restored creation in an existence of rich abundance. Fear has been replaced by peace and prosperity.

> Be not afraid, O land;
> be glad and rejoice.
> Surely the Lord has done great things.
> Be not afraid, O wild animals,
> for the open pastures are becoming green.
> The trees are bearing their fruit;
> the fig tree and the vine yield their riches.
> Be glad, O people of Zion,
> rejoice in the Lord your God,
> for he has given you
> the autumn rains in righteousness.
> He sends you abundant showers,
> both autumn and spring rains, as before.
> The threshing floors will be filled with grain;
> the vats will overflow with new wine and oil.
> *(Joel 2:21-24)*

Joel is giving God's response to a plea for mercy. If the people truly repent, God promises restoration, rest, and protection, as well as benefits to the natural world. God through Joel addresses the land and the beasts, talks of the yield of the fig tree and vine, and the coming rains. The renewed rain is another outward symbol of an inward reality, the restored fellowship with God. The arrival of the rain demonstrates God's blessing on the heart now properly prepared for him. Joel concludes the passage with the promise that God's people will experience the abiding presence of God himself, dwelling in their midst.[1]

The sequence of thought starts with restoring first the harmony between humans and God, then between creation and God. The ultimate result is the promise of God's presence.

## Restoration of the Natural World and the Promised Spirit

The passages tell of restoration of the physical world after the coming of something new—the Spirit.

> The fortress will be abandoned,
>    the noisy city deserted;
> citadel and watchtower will become a wasteland
>       forever,
>    the delight of donkeys, a pasture for flocks,
> till the Spirit is poured upon us from on high,
>    and the desert becomes a fertile field,
>    and the fertile field seems like a forest.
> Justice will dwell in the desert
>    and righteousness live in the fertile field.
>
> *(Isa. 32:14-16)*

The outpouring of the Spirit precedes the promised abundance of nature, turning a wasteland into pastures and fertile fields. That same Spirit is available to Christians as they minister in Jesus' name.

> For I will pour water on the thirsty land,
>    and streams on the dry ground;
> I will pour out my Spirit on your offspring,
>    and my blessing on your descendants.
> They will spring up like grass in a meadow,
>    like poplar trees by flowing streams. *(Isa. 44:3-4)*

Isaiah foretold it, and later Ezekiel captured the vision of God's work. He wrote that the people will be given a new heart and a new spirit. Then as God's people, we will see the end of famine, the end of desolation. The earth will be "like the garden of Eden."

I will give you a new heart and put a new spirit in you; I will remove from you your heart of stone and give you a heart of flesh. And I will put my Spirit in you. . . . They will say, "This land that was laid waste has become like the garden of Eden." . . . I the Lord have spoken, and I will do it. *(Ezek. 36:26-27, 35-36)*

The most important result of Israel's restoration would be the spread of the knowledge of the Lord throughout the world. The nations would unequivocally know that Israel's God had accomplished this restoration. They would know that Israel's God was not weak but the only God to be trusted to follow through precisely as promised.[2]

## The Natural World and Salvation

Our salvation comes from God Almighty, a salvation for the whole creation.

But you, O God, are my king from of old;.
    you bring salvation upon the earth.
It was you who split open the sea by your power. . . .
It was you who opened up springs and streams;
    you dried up the ever flowing rivers.
The day is yours, and yours also the night;
    you established the sun and moon.
It was you who set all the boundaries of the earth;
    you made both summer and winter. *(Ps. 74:12-17)*

Here the poet again weaves together the Bible's salvation and creation themes. The God of Israel overcomes all hostile powers to redeem the people and establish a new order in the world. God alone can effect redemption and establish his kingdom in the world against all opposition.

## The Natural World and Reconciliation

For God so loved the world that he gave his only Son.
*(John 3:16, NRSV)*

The salvation for humanity was assured with the coming of Jesus Christ. That salvation was extended to the creation.

He rescued us from the domain of darkness and brought us away into the kingdom of his dear Son, in whom our release is secured and our sins forgiven. . . . Through him God chose to reconcile the whole universe to himself, making peace through the shedding of his blood upon the cross—to reconcile all things, whether on earth or in heaven, through him alone.
*(Col. 1:13-14, 20, NEB)*

Jesus Christ was a historical figure, showing us through personal sacrifice, example, and teaching, the way back to the Creator. This way is open to anyone who believes, yet it is a personal pathway. Focused and narrow, it leads to life (Matt. 7:14). It has the power to turn us toward wholeness, both inwardly and outwardly.

Christianity is a spiritual walk that has been field-tested for two thousand years. Scripture documents the mystery of the Creator, gives guidelines for communing with God, and instructs us in maintaining a Spirit-led life. The Testaments relate stories of the people who have followed the way of the Lord, offering examples and guidance for us.

The Christian system at its best gives meaning to life, promoting understanding, intellectual satisfaction, fulfillment in service and peace. It is a way of life evident in daily experience as the ongoing gift from God, who loves us.

It is difficult to convey in words the added dimension that this spiritual experience brings to the believer. Until they experience the hand of God in their own life, people struggle to understand why Spirit-led Christians are so enthusiastic and excited. Living by the grace of God unfolds a daily adventure for the believer, a life of rich relationships, expectancy, great fulfillment and hope.

God's purposes can focus our existence as well as that of the entire creation. An abundant natural world and a human population living in harmony and communion with the Creator will result in great joy and peace.

## The Natural World Will Be Redeemed

The Lord God created a good universe and earth. Sin came into the world as Satan and the celestial host who followed him tempted humans, who succumbed.

With one exception, all humans have been separated from God through sin. The effect, according to Scripture, is not only to bring evil into the lives of people, but into all nature. As a result, many Christians tend to separate themselves from nature because they view the natural world as hopelessly evil, hopelessly lost.

Nothing could be further from the truth, Paul says in his message to the Romans. We are to remain full of joyful hope, assured by the promise of our God that not only are nature and humanity to be redeemed, but the universe as well. According to Paul's letter to the Romans, the physical universe is not destined for destruction, but for renewal. Living things will no longer be subject to death and decay, as they are today.[3]

> I consider that the sufferings of this present time are not worth comparing with the glory about to be revealed to us. For the creation waits with eager longing for the revealing of the children of God; for the creation was subjected to futility, not of its own will but

by the will of the one who subjected it, in hope that the
creation itself will be set free from its bondage to decay
and will obtain the freedom of the glory of the children
of God. We know that the whole creation has been
groaning in labor pains until now; and not only the
creation, but we ourselves, who have the first fruits of
the Spirit, groan inwardly while we wait for adoption,
the redemption of our bodies. *(Rom. 8:18-23, NRSV)*

Paul goes on to affirm that God calls us according to his
design and purpose (Rom. 8:28). Our role is to advance
that purpose.

## The Promised New Heaven and New Earth

Behold, I will create new heavens and a new earth.
The former things will not be remembered,
      nor will they come to mind.
But be glad and rejoice forever in what I will create. . . .
                                        *(Isa. 65:17-18)*

The promise of a new heaven and a new earth echoes
the Old Testament prophet Isaiah. Later John envisioned
this new heaven and new earth in his great Revelation.

Then I saw a new heaven and a new earth; for the first
heaven and the first earth had passed away, and the sea
was no more. And I saw the holy city, the new
Jerusalem, coming down out of heaven from God,
prepared as a bride adorned for her husband. And I
heard a loud voice from the throne saying,
      "See, the home of God is
         among mortals.
      He will dwell with them as
         their God;

they will be his peoples,
and God himself will be with
  them. . . . *(Rev. 21:1-3, NRSV)*

This apocalyptic vision is one of great glory and joy. That God will dwell with people is an astonishing and humbling prediction. Will we be ready? Will the creation be ready?

God is quoted repeatedly as saying, "I will do it!" in regard to creating the new heaven and new earth, and restoring the land. As a result some Christians think they have no responsibility. These Christians choose to leave everything to God. This is a limited viewpoint, foreign to the way Christianity works. While it is true that God's sovereign plan for the earth and humanity will prevail, God accomplishes much of the work through his servants.

We must raise the question, when does redemption begin? The answer lies in the act of deliverance. Through knowledge of the life, ministry, death, and resurrection of Jesus Christ, we come to realize that it is through Jesus we are redeemed. Through the witness of the Gospel writings, we understand the resurrection as God's climactic redemptive work through Jesus Christ. When we accept Jesus Christ as a personal Savior and ask forgiveness of our sins, we are accepted; God forgives us, delivering us from the guilt and power of sin.

This act is personal and individual. Yet Jesus called not just individuals, but a new people to follow him. When we as individuals come to Christ, we also join a group, a people that follows the teachings and commands of Jesus Christ. Jesus is not only Savior, but also Lord and Master.

As a result of deliverance, we are free to enjoy the whole life of the Spirit of God. This entails a life of peace, freedom, responsibility, compassion. Such a life yields love, meekness, patience, long-suffering, self-control, and the strength to serve God. "Man has not been accounted righteous in some distant world, but here and now *in the Church*, and in and for our world." [4]

What a waste it would be to wait for the "new heaven and the new earth." The new life we are promised as Christians begins at salvation and starts here on earth. Redemption for Christians and for the creation begins now.

Christians strive for a life of righteousness, living in harmony with God and extending that harmony to the natural world insofar as possible. When it comes to doing God's work, we are the hands, we are the feet.

## Questions for Discussion

1. How does the Creation relate to redemption?

2. What does it mean to have a "new heart and a new spirit"? How is that related to the redemption of the natural world?

3. What will reconciliation mean for the whole creation?

4. When does redemption begin? For us? For the creation?

# 11. The Natural World and Praise

PRAISE is a major biblical theme. When we praise we commend the worth of someone or something; we express approval or admiration. Praise is part of our prayerful response to the living God.

When directed toward God, praise becomes a form of worship. This praise focuses the feelings that well up within us when we experience God's love. We laud God's being with extravagant words and gestures. Using poetry, song, movement, or other expression, we sing, shout, clap, dance and extol God's name. The glory and majesty of God, and the marvel of the Maker's works, move us to praise of overwhelming joy and thanksgiving.

In Scripture, the natural world joins the praise to God. From the Psalms to Revelation, all creatures—as well as the sun, moon, stars, and other forms of creation—are expected to praise God.

## The Natural World Is Commanded to Praise God

Humanity and the whole creation are told to praise God in everything and at every opportunity. This charge is repeated again and again throughout the Scriptures. The earth is to be a place of praise.

Make a joyful noise to God, all
the earth;
sing the glory of his name;
give to him glorious praise.
Say to God, "How awesome are
your deeds!
Because of your great power,
your enemies cringe before
you.
All the earth worships you;
they sing praises to you,
sing praises to your name. *(Ps. 66:1-4, NRSV)*

Praise the Lord!
Praise the Lord from the heavens,
praise him in the heights!
Praise him, all his angels,
praise him, all his host!

Praise him, sun and moon;
praise him, all you shining stars!
Praise him, you highest heavens
and you waters above the heavens! . . .

Praise the Lord from the earth
you sea monsters and all the deeps,
fire and hail, snow and frost,
stormy wind fulfilling his command!

Mountains and all hills,
    fruit trees and all cedars,
Wild animals and all cattle,
    creeping things and flying birds!

Kings of the earth and all peoples,
    princes and all rulers on earth!
Young men and women alike,
    old and young together!

    Let them praise the name of the Lord,
        for his name alone is exalted.
    His glory is above earth and heaven.
                    *(Ps. 148:1-4, 7-13, NRSV)*

In another passage Isaiah speaks of mountains and hills that burst into song, trees of the field that will clap their hands (Isa. 55:12). When we experience moments of great beauty outdoors, we feel the joy and exhilaration of the natural world around us. Surely these are moments of praise to God. All creation joins with the celebration of God's goodness in the natural world, in blessing, and in redemption.

## Reasons to Praise the Lord

We praise God for who God is, thanking the Lord for what he does. The Psalms in particular are filled with reasons to praise God and reminders to do so.

The Lord is righteous in all his ways
    and loving toward all he has made.
The Lord is near to all who call on him. . . .
He fulfills the desires of those who fear him. . . .
The Lord watches over all who love him. . . .

My mouth will speak in praise of the Lord.
Let every creature praise his holy name
for ever and ever. *(Ps. 145:17-21)*

Praise him for his acts of power;
praise him for his surpassing greatness. *(Ps. 150:2)*

The ancient Israelites were commanded to praise God for the good land.

Observe the commands of the Lord your God, walking in his ways and revering him. For the Lord your God is bringing you into a good land—a land with streams and pools of water, with springs flowing in the valleys and hills. . . .
When you have eaten and are satisfied, praise the Lord your God for the good land he has given you. Be careful that you do not forget the Lord your God."
*(Deut. 8:6-7, 10-11)*

Praising God also yields blessings from the earth.

May the peoples praise you, O God;
may all the peoples praise you.
Then the land will yield its harvest,
and God, our God, will bless us.
God will bless us,
and all the ends of the earth will fear him.
*(Ps. 67:5-7)*

Praising God for his all-abiding power, beauty, and goodness, we affirm our faith and belief in the Almighty. When we draw close to God, we are blessed by God in many ways, including the blessings of the land that result in a fruitful harvest.

## The Principle of Praise

Praise becomes a spiritual principle, an essential element of our worship of God that not only celebrates the character and magnitude of the Lord but produces surprising results.

The most obvious outcome of our praise to God is that it draws us closer to the Creator. By praising God we establish a means of communication, opening up a way to reach the Lord.

> Rejoice in the Lord always. I will say it again: Rejoice!
> Let your gentleness be evident to all. The Lord is near.
> Do not be anxious about anything, but in everything by
> prayer and petition, with thanksgiving, present your
> requests to God.                           *(Phil. 4:4-6)*

The many commands to praise God are not always easy to follow. At a given moment, a person may not be inspired to join the praise. However, if we do not praise God "always," we withhold from the Lord what rightfully belongs to God's glory. At times the righteous person assumes praise as a duty, and in this there is a sound psychological principle. When we begin the act of praise, the emotion lacking may return. At the least we are likely to experience release from the spiritual tensions that hinder us.

> Through Jesus, therefore, let us continually offer to
> God a sacrifice of praise—the fruit of lips that confess
> his name.                                  *(Heb. 13:15)*

We are called to praise God sometimes in the face of circumstances that are not so fortunate. In this imperfect world there are times when things go wrong, our prayers are seemingly unanswered, and God remains distant. A prayer of praise may seem impossible, yet it may be the only thing left to do. At this point our praise becomes a sacrifice to God.

When we set aside our troubles and acknowledge the sovereignty of the Lord, we may feel we are denying a painful problem. Yet this may be the quickest way to reach God, for a sacrifice of praise in a troublesome situation can become the most powerful prayer of all. In the words of Catherine Marshall, "This is because praise is faith in action, faith in its most vigorous form." We are acting out our belief in the power and presence of God.[1]

> Though the fig tree does not bud
> and there are no grapes on the vines,
> though the olive crop fails
> and the fields produce no food,
> though there are no sheep in the pen
> and no cattle in the stalls,
> yet I will rejoice in the Lord,
> I will be joyful in God my Savior. *(Hab. 3:17-18)*

This remarkable statement in Habakkuk affirms belief in the sovereignty of God and absolute trust in divine ways.

Praise is an important key to communing with God. We are taught in Scripture that the Lord lives in our praises.

> Holy One, you
> who make your home in the praises of Israel . . .
> *(Ps. 22:3, JB)*

We exalt God for his power and presence and because of the mighty deeds performed for God's people. God makes his home in our praises, and we may be touched by the presence of God.

## The Earth Is to Be a Place of Praise

The psalmist included the creation in the praising of the Lord. Today we can see the work of dedicated gardeners and conservationists. In the cultivated gardens and fields, as well as the many preserved and restored habitat and wilderness areas, we can find a natural world that seems to praise the Creator.

> The grasslands of the desert overflow;
> the hills are clothed with gladness.
> The meadows are covered with flocks
> and the valleys are mantled with grain;
> they shout for joy and sing. *(Ps. 65:12-13)*

> Let the heavens rejoice, let the earth be glad;
> let the sea resound, and all that is in it;
> let the fields be jubilant, and everything in them.
> Then all the trees of the forest will sing for joy;
> they will sing before the Lord, for he comes. . . .
> *(Ps. 96:11-13)*

> Praise the Lord, all his works
> everywhere in his dominion. *(Ps. 103:22)*

> Let everything that has breath praise the Lord.
> *(Ps. 150:6)*

The writers of Scripture had experienced those moments of beauty when the natural world responds to the Creator.

When John had his great vision of Revelation, he saw that day, now arriving but not yet here in its fullness, when all creatures will praise God and sing! He painted a glorious picture of God's restoration, the end result of redemption and reconciliation, in which the whole earth will be once again in harmony with the Lord, a harmony that will be *heard.*

> Then I heard every creature in heaven and on earth
> and under the earth and on the sea, and all that is in
> them, singing:
>     "To him who sits on the throne and to the Lamb
>     be praise and honor and glory and power,
>         forever and ever!" *(Rev. 5:13)*

The earth is to be a place of praise, but the sad truth is that much of the land has been spoiled. Because of our negligence and exploitation we hinder the land from doing the work of sustaining us and other of God's creatures. We also hinder the land's role in praising God. We exploit people; we are out of harmony with ourselves; we are out of harmony with nature—all because we are out of harmony with God.

It is intriguing to speculate on just what the music will sound like when all creatures praise the Lord. What kind of music will be pleasing to the Lord of creation? The sounds of the Bushman and Pygmy peoples who live close to the source of humanity's known beginnings are reported to have a music that might have come from the "Garden of Eden." Their music reflects their way of life in a society that is complementary, chiefless, egalitarian, and pacifist. Men and women, old and young, are linked in close interdependence by preference and not by force. Variants of this style are found the world over among primitive peoples who still live in direct harmony with the earth.[2] The harmony they have achieved is seemingly expressed in their music.

In general, the sound of our singing reflects our well-being. It reflects our condition in terms of inward peace and outward justice. Given varying degrees of talent, the quality of the sound itself can become the very music of our lives. If we are out of harmony, the singing of praise can be difficult and discordant.

Restoring that harmony means forming a new relationship with God through Jesus Christ. Restoring harmony with God is the first step to renewal—personally, publicly, and as extended to the environment.

When our relationship with God is resonant and true, we can work toward justice for all peoples and the natural world. Freedom from oppression, freedom from strife, freedom from want will contribute to a new harmony. Then we can be in tune with each other in every way as well as in tune with the natural world, singing praise to God at every opportunity.

For the heavenly choir that still sits in the pews at home, practicing songs and hymns of praise is good preparation for what is to come. Then perhaps the community of Christ will come closer to sounding the harmony that God expects in the new heaven and the new earth.

## Questions for Discussion

1. Define praise. How does the natural world praise God?

2. Why do we praise God?

3. Why is praise important?

4. How can we praise God always? How do we praise when things to wrong?

5. How do you imagine the earth in the time to come when it is fully transformed into a place of praise?

# 12. The Natural World and Glory

OUR human definitions of glory fall short when we try to explain the glory of God. People equate glory with great honor and admiration, even fame, and for people, this is valid. But the human notion of glory is not the same as the glory of the Lord.

To *glorify* is to praise and exalt, which we express in our worship. But the *glory* of God is a concept of vast spiritual dimension. We find clues in the Scriptures, descriptions that illustrate God's glory, which is described as light, a rainbow, brightness, a divine attribute of illustriousness and eminence. However, scriptural descriptions are like the tip of an iceberg, revealing just a small portion of the real thing. We learn that God's glory is more than a visual display; it is an experience.

We note that God's glory is connected with the natural world, since it is revealed through natural means. In addition the earth has a purpose in terms of God's glory, an important point to remember as we care for the environment.

## Descriptions of the Glory of God

Natural phenomena are used throughout the Bible to describe the glory of God. This glory was revealed to the Israelites as a cloud by day and a pillar of fire by night.

> Then the cloud covered the Tent of Meeting, and the glory of the Lord filled the tabernacle. Moses could not enter the Tent of Meeting because the cloud had settled upon it, and the glory of the Lord filled the tabernacle. . . . So the cloud of the Lord was over the tabernacle by day, and fire was in the cloud by night, in the sight of all the house of Israel during all their travels.
> *(Exod. 40:34-35, 38)*

When the ark of the covenant was brought into the temple that Solomon built, the glory of the Lord was overwhelming.

> When the priests withdrew from the Holy Place, the cloud filled the temple of the Lord. And the priests could not perform their service because of the cloud, for the glory of the Lord filled his temple.
> *(1 Kings 8:10-11)*

Ezekiel too was overwhelmed by a vision of the glory of God, a vision of dazzling radiance.

> . . . Brilliant light surrounded him. Like the appearance of a rainbow in the clouds on a rainy day, so was the radiance around him.

> This was the appearance of the likeness of the glory
> of the Lord. When I saw it, I fell facedown. . . .
>
> *(Ezek. 1:27-28)*

Postema defines the glory of the Lord as the active presence of God.[1] When God's glory appears, in whatever form, the experience is undeniable and overwhelming for those present. Such an experience has triggered extraordinary performance on the part of some. Moses defied a Pharaoh and led the Israelites through the long wilderness journey. Isaiah was cleansed and responded to the Lord, "Send me!" Paul dramatically changed his life from persecuting Christians to spreading the gospel.

> And the Word became flesh and lived among us, and
> we have seen his glory, the glory as of a father's only
> son, full of grace and truth. *(John 1:14, NRSV)*

The glory of God was seen in Jesus Christ. The people who experienced that glory were transformed, moving into a life of active discipleship and service that has changed the world.

## The Natural World Declares God's Glory

From the awesome splendor of the universe to the beauty and structure of the dynamic system, the whole creation is used to reflect God's glory.

> The heavens are telling the glory of God;
>    and the firmament proclaims his handiwork.
> Day to day pours forth speech,
>    and night to night declares knowledge.
> There is no speech, nor are there words;
>    their voice is not heard;

yet their voice goes out through all the earth,
and their words to the end of the world.

(Ps. 19:1-4, NRSV)

The glory in the creation testifies to the righteousness and faithfulness of the Lord who owns it.

## Humans Were Formed for God's Glory

The human soul has great worth. The value of each individual is affirmed in Isaiah's humbling insight.

Bring my sons from afar
    and my daughters from the ends of the earth—
everyone who is called by my name,
    whom I created for my glory,
    whom I formed and made. *(Isa. 43:6-7)*

This astonishing statement brings home the truth of God's love for each individual. Humans are part of the creation. We have a purpose. We are formed for God's glory. How can we fail to respond to this great love?

## The Glory of the Lord Will Fill the Earth

For Christians, the goal of a mature spiritual life is the glory of God. Although a gift of grace, our praise to God may call up this glory.

The whole earth is also to be filled with the glory of God. The Scriptures reveal a major purpose for the planet —the earth and everything in it is planned for God's glory. The caring Creator formed a dwelling place.

. . . and as surely as the glory of the Lord fills the whole earth. . . *(Num. 14:21)*

Since those ancient times, the Lord's glory on earth is mentioned in future terms.

Praise be to the Lord God, the God of Israel,
   who alone does marvelous deeds.
Praise be to his glorious name forever;
   may the whole earth be filled with his glory.
      Amen and amen. *(Ps. 72:18-19)*

Biblical writers have told of glory extensive enough to fill the whole earth. Isaiah shared such a vision.

And they were calling to one another;
"Holy, holy, holy is the Lord Almighty;
the whole earth is full of his glory." *(Isa. 6:3)*

All creation is called to praise. When the natural world is restored, we will praise God anew, with hope and expectation, as promised in Habakkuk.

For the earth will be filled with the knowledge of the
      glory of the Lord,
   as the waters cover the sea. *(Hab. 2:14)*

## Questions for Discussion

1. What is the glory of God? How has it been manifested on earth?

2. Why were humans formed?

3. Discuss the promise that "the whole earth will be filled with the glory of the Lord" (Hab. 2:14). What will the earth be like? What does this mean for us as Christians?

# PART 3

## Earth
## Stewardship

# 13. The Earth Is Suffering

A GLANCE through the contents of one of the many environmental handbooks reveals an appalling list of environmental troubles:

Degradation of croplands
Soil erosion
Pesticide poisoning
Desertification of grazing lands
Deforestation
Diminished yields in fisheries
Reliance on nonrenewable fossil fuels
Depletion of nonrenewable minerals
Acid rain
Air pollution
Global warming
Ozone depletion

Ruined marine zones
Polluted oceans and waterways
Decreasing groundwater supplies
Unsafe drinking water
Materials wasted
Poisons released
Municipal waste
Hazardous waste
Decreasing wildlife
Overharvest of whales
"Factory" farming practices for poultry, calves,
    and hogs
Species extinction
Human overpopulation
Overcultivating
Overgrazing
Overcutting
Overfishing

The scope of the problems is staggering. The causes and effects cross nations, oceans, and international boundaries. The dangers extend around the globe in an interlocking network of potential disasters.

In the nine hundred days it took a United Nations commission to compile *Our Common Future*, the report of the World Commission on Environment and Development, an alarming number of calamities occurred.

1. The drought-triggered, environment-development crisis in Africa peaked, affecting 35 million people and killing perhaps a million.

2. A leak from a pesticides factory in Bhopal, India, killed more than two thousand people and blinded and injured over two hundred thousand more.

3. Liquid gas tanks exploded in Mexico City, killing one

thousand and leaving thousands more homeless.

4. The Chernobyl nuclear reactor explosion sent nuclear fallout across Europe, increasing the risks of future human cancers, as well as making a section of the creation uninhabitable.

5. Agricultural chemicals, solvents, and mercury flowed into the Rhine River during a warehouse fire in Switzerland, killing millions of fish and threatening drinking water in the Federal Republic of Germany and the Netherlands.

6. An estimated 60 million people died of diarrheal diseases related to unsafe drinking water and malnutrition; most of the victims were children.

This United Nations report also states that it is impossible to separate economic development issues from environmental issues. Many forms of development erode the very environmental resources upon which they must be based. Conversely, environmental degradation can undermine economic development. The report lists poverty as a major cause and effect of global environmental problems. Therefore, it is futile to attempt to deal with economic problems without also dealing with the environmental.[1]

When we think of the problems as global, it is too easy to believe the problems are somewhere else. But in fact, the global problems lie right on our doorstep. It has become painfully clear that, like the woodsman who strives unsuccessfully to leave no tracks, every move we make has some effect on the environment. Every product we use has made some demand on world resources.

Our common acts of daily life affect people elsewhere on the globe, and they affect generations yet unborn.

## *The Work*

The first inhabitants of the earth inherited a literal paradise; but with paradise came responsibility. People were given the specific task of taking care of the earth.

> God blessed them and said to them, "Be fruitful and increase in number; fill the earth and subdue it.
>
> *(Gen. 1:28a)*

Christians have been blamed for environmental problems because of this Scripture verse, but in fact most of the earth's peoples share in the causes of destruction.

Human cultures flourish and turn decadent. Wars lay waste vast tracts of land. Human populations have increased in number until the earth is overfull, and untold millions of people are either malnourished or actually starving. In some areas there are so many people that their very presence destroys the environment. Civilizations have "subdued," that is, "taken by force," the earth's resources and devastated habitats everywhere.

The Hebrew word for *subdue*, while forceful, does not mean wanton destruction. We are to use the earth's resources, be fruitful, and replenish, not just in terms of human population, but in terms of all life forms.

The line between use and misuse is narrow and elusive. In order to live we must use the resources and fruits of the earth, but without taking too much. Finding the optimum balance between need and supply is one challenge. Another challenge is to face our spiritual impoverishment.

> The earth dries up and withers,
>> the world languishes and withers,
>> the exalted of the earth languish.
> The earth is defiled by its people;
>> they have disobeyed the laws,

violated the statues
and broken the everlasting covenant. *(Isa. 24:4-5)*

In ancient times Isaiah connected the condition of the
earth with the sins and shortcomings of the people. This is
also a contemporary problem. We too are often estranged
from God. Bereft of God's Holy Spirit, we live outside
God's plan and purpose, to our detriment and the detriment of the earth. To be healed, we must return to God,
seeking a close relationship through Jesus Christ. Then we
can get on with the problems of the earth.

Spiritual poverty is one flaw. A lack of biological
knowledge is another. In the words of Art and Jocele Meyer, in their book *Earthkeepers,*

> Most present economic systems—capitalist, communist,
> or socialist—disregard fundamental laws of nature. They
> pay little attention to ecological principles, such as "every-
> thing is connected to everything else," "everything must
> go somewhere," "nature knows best," and "there is no
> such thing as a free lunch." Because of this disregard, our
> societies are building up dangerous environmental debts.
> Present political-economic systems promote an untenable
> free-lunch mentality. When implemented, these systems
> exploit nature or people or both.[2]

Urgently needed are remedies for the acute results of
overpopulation, overuse, and destruction. But to stop environmental troubles, our earth management and lifestyle
practices must change. Until we understand the workings
of the natural world, comprehend its complex systems,
and fit our daily living patterns into those systems, we will
continue to work not *with* but *against* nature's ways.

Scripture does not direct us to leave the earth alone.
Nor are we commanded to use it up. We are directed to
help it flourish.

## *A Christian Viewpoint*

The creation Scriptures show the many ways that God's natural world is threaded into the biblical narrative. The natural world is linked to every major theme of the Christian faith. The passages are familiar. We hear them read at weekly worship services, but we tune out references to the natural world and heed the text only as it relates to people.

Because the creation themes are muted for the most part, they are easy to ignore. In addition, our viewpoint is so often self-centered rather than God-centered that we have not seen the importance of the original vocation that God gave us. We have failed to include the earth as part of God's work.

Our God declared the natural world to be good. Some religions and philosophies set forth a totally different view. Although contrary to a biblical viewpoint, these philosophies still influence Western thinking.

Greco-Roman philosophical schools, such as hermeticism, asceticism, Stoicism, and gnosticism, declared a dualism which regarded spirit as good and matter as evil. Not only is this the opposite of what we know from Genesis about the natural world, but dualism in itself is not recognized by Christians, since good and evil are not understood to be equal. An infinite God who is good outweighs evil in influence and extent.

Within the Christian community, there has been misunderstanding of the goodness of creation. This was evident in the monastic emphasis on separation from the world during the pre-Reformation era. This was also evident in the pietistic movement, wherein there was a tendency to identify evil with things rather than with the misuse of things.[3]

Some Eastern religions stress the cultivation of the inner self through meditation and contemplation. Rightly understood, Eastern tendencies don't necessarily lead to a turning away from the earth, since much Eastern thought calls the individual to a form of deep centering which leads toward careful awareness of all life. Yet some strands of Eastern thought have sometimes influenced individuals to focus entirely onto themselves and away from the world and its problems.

In Christian contemplation, the goal is not simply to cultivate the inner self. The fully lived Christian life brings assessment of one's capabilities and continuing personal growth, so that we might know who we are and what we can offer in God's service. Christians meditate to develop deeper grounding in God from which to draw strength as they address the needs of the outer world.

According to Paulos Mar Gregorios in his essay, "New Testament Foundations for Understanding the Creation,"

> Even when we are thinking about the environment or socio-economic and political life. . . . We should focus our minds and wills on the higher realities (Col. 3:1-2) (not the inner), which must be manifested in the earthly realities—now partially, but in the end, fully.[4]

True Christian contemplation is always lived out in service.

Some ancient religions view the earth as sacred, adopting rituals wherein various natural forms, living and non-living, are objects of worship. Feeling a sense of community with the earth, we recognize the common thread we share with God's created world. We are made by the same divine hand, with similar design limitations, and in abundant variety. Yet nowhere in Scripture are the earth forms called "sacred," except when associated with God in a particular circumstance, such as the burning bush in the story of Moses (Exod. 3:2).

Building a spirituality around the mysteries of the earth and calling the earth "sacramental" is not biblical, nor does it acknowledge the lessons of biology. Nature on the whole is good, but there is the problem of natural evil. Natural disasters, the vagaries of wind and weather, aggressive behaviors, accidents, and unhappy circumstances must be taken into account. Those who live through natural calamities would scarcely deem them sacred acts. The Christian view supports the eventual redemption of the creation, "a new heaven and a new earth."

The physical world is the expression of the Creator God. We value and care for the masterpieces of a Michelangelo or a Rembrandt. Yet we know that the paint, the paper, the canvas, the marble, the composition are extraordinary work but are not the person; they are, rather, an expression of the artist. Likewise God's Creation was a divine act but the objects created are not themselves divine. At the same time, however, we must cherish the forms and objects which make up the physical world. Otherwise we destroy the expression of God as surely as we destroy the expressions of great artists if we mutilate their paintings.

In Genesis the first thing God said to humans was basically, "Here's the earth. Take care of it" (Gen. 1:28-29). This is restated in Genesis 2:15 and paraphrased in Psalm 8:6-8. Throughout the rest of the Bible, references to the natural world are mostly indirect. The writers assume the original command and thread the creation vocabulary into their writings as one more strand in the whole of God's work.

Theologians now hone the fine points of environmental theology. Human dominion of the earth has taken on an ugly tone. This is because it has become equated with domination which separates humans from nature, allows oppression of other humans as well as the natural world, and has been exercised without benefit of the Creator's guidance. But even though now unfashionable as an ethic, humans still live "dominion of the earth" in practice. Lifestyles and economies are based on the faulty assumption that the earth is a resource to be exploited.[5]

Because of this, many Christians are calling for stewardship of the earth. Yet the "stewards" of God struggle with how much autonomy is right. Rising too far above nature—or staying too distant from God—can be detrimental to good earthkeeping.

Those who say we are "partners" with God affirm human dignity, yet agree we are part of nature not above or outside it. As part of nature, humans confirm that sense of community we share with the physical world and validate the integrity of all parts of the creation, from the smallest amoeba to towering cliffs that rise from the sea. Saint Francis modeled such a view, loving the earth and adopting a simple way of life more suited to environmental constraints.

Scientists have voiced urgent concerns about the well-being of the planet. In a discussion of Christian models for environmental work, Larry Rasmussen notes,

> The cause of the eco-crisis is twofold: (1) We are living in ways that outstrip nature's capacity to regenerate itself on its own time cycles and terms. (2) We are forcing changes in natural systems themselves—changes inhospitable even to species with considerable adaptability. This is why *"sustainability"* is the crucial minimum criterion for all forms of life.[6]

The scientific assessment must be taken seriously by Christians. Christian beliefs then offer the unifying focus, the dependable guidance, the disciplines, and the service motivated by love of God that can make a difference.

The environmental crisis has called forth diverse groups within the Christian community. Indigenous peoples, social activists, feminists, and members of cultural groups from around the globe are facing the issues and joining the struggle for solutions. Individual and communal assessment brings forth dismay and horror at the extensive damage to the earth, closely followed by deep concern and caring for what happens to God's creation. Prophetic voices are being raised, calling us back to God before it is too late; calling for a true conversion, away from both spiritually and physically destructive ways of life.

We need not support underlying philosophies—such as New Age thinking—of all who are concerned about the environment. Yet too often we Christians let doctrinal debates stop us from getting on with the real work of the Lord. We also let quarrels between science and religion overwhelm our common sense. The quarrels needlessly alienate Christian scientists, gardeners, and naturalists, those very specialists we need in the environmental ministry.

Theological discussion is needed on the environmental issues, yet it is time-consuming. Because we know the importance of the natural world to Christian principles, and because of the precarious state of the environment, we would be foolish to withhold action while working to refine doctrine.

We have a basic motive for earthkeeping—the Creator God was first revealed to the ancient Hebrews through their experience with nature. That alone validates its importance to the Christian faith. We have a particular reason for preserving and renewing the earth, a particular reason for wanting the natural world to continue that same work. Because of the beauty and grand design of the natural world, other people might make the same discovery.

The Scriptures give the second major reason to care for the earth, telling us things about the Creator God that go beyond what the natural world reveals. The natural imagery lends meaning and message to Scriptural truths. Through the writings of the prophets we have learned that

(1) God has plans and purposes for the earth, (2) God blessed life, and (3) God gave the care of the planet into our hands.

A third reason to care for the earth is the coming of Jesus Christ. The world was loved and valued so much that God sent his only Son to save it. Jesus used the natural world to teach and minister. In his death and resurrection, he provided redemption not only for his people but for creation as well.

At the heart of the matter we recognize God's sovereign will. The earth and everything in it comes under the all-abiding plan and sovereignty of God. As God's people we know, as Friesen states, that "God's sovereignty does not exclude the need for *planning*; it does require humble submission to his will." [7]

God calls us first to commitment to God through a personal relationship with Jesus Christ; and second, to our vocation to the earth, a vocation that includes people. We know that the environment benefits when humans become God's people and develop spiritually. We are accountable for our gifts, our talents, our way of life. We are expected to use our hearts, brains, and abilities, so we can act compassionately, justly, knowledgeably, and effectively. As Christians we work to accomplish God's will.

The key to operation earthkeeping is seeking God's will at all times. For this, the Christian takes needs, problems, and even solutions to God in prayer. Through contemplation, study, and consultation, it is possible to discern the right solutions. Then in God's timing we can move forward in confidence as the Holy Spirit works through us to accomplish God's work.

## A Call to Action

If God is holding an environmental scorecard, it is easy to see our team is not doing well. Our polluted waterways, fouled air, ruined land, destruction of plant and animal life, famine, disease, and human overpopulation are the glaring results of our greed, inattention, and ignorance. Our very lifestyles impair the earth.

Many well-meaning and compassionate Christians have simply not been aware of the problems and needs of the earth itself until now. Good people have not remembered that Christian faith is rooted in the acts of the Creator God. And they have not seen how their faith heritage underscores the importance of the natural world. Pastors and lay people alike are now facing the Christian responsibility for the planet.

The problems on a worldwide basis seem overwhelming. Can one person really make a difference? Can groups scattered over the world have any impact on the environmental needs, sway the opinions of those in political power, or outweigh the greed that grips the economies of small communities and great nations?

We can only point to the overall increase of good in the world. Even though evil is still rampant, the human population continues to make slow progress. In the twentieth century, we have seen major medical miracles, such as the eradication of smallpox. The world no longer has slavery as a government-approved social institution. And most Christians are surprised to hear that Christianity is the most widespread and largest growing religion in the world, with a membership of fully one-third of the world's population.[8]

Paul Brand tells a story of how the vision and persistent tree-planting of one doctor transformed a barren gravel, nearly waterless site for a new hospital in India, into a sanctuary of beauty and healing.

Ernest made a rule for himself that every year he would plant trees and more trees. To follow his rule, he collected seeds and seedlings from everywhere and nourished them in his own garden until they were strong. Then he planted them just before the rains, and had them watered by staff and patients until they had root systems deep enough to survive. . . . I remember the hospital and the staff houses and chapel that grew up around it. They were gray and white and stood out against the skyline. They were the only structures to break the monotony of the gravel slopes for miles. When I approach that hospital today, it is invisible, hidden in a forest that is higher than the tallest buildings. The place has been declared a sanctuary by the Environmental Department of the government. The whole area is full of birds; we counted and identified about forty species in one afternoon. The water table, which is falling in most places, was rising last year under the gravel at Karagiri. Soil is being built up, not lost.[9]

Can we make a difference? The answer is an emphatic yes. With a Christ-centered ministry, each individual is important in contributing to the accomplishment of God's plans.

A Christian call to action, then, will cover these main points.

1. We seek God's will and guidance as we plan our strategies. This is a call to prayer.

2. Human spiritual life is related to environmental health. Both are Christian concerns.

3. The results of environmental damage must be healed, while at the same time the sources of damage must be eliminated.

4. The problems are global and also individual. Changes must be made on every side—home, community, region, nation, world, and outer space.

5. The economy and the ecology go hand in hand, and

strategies for one cannot be separated from the other; social justice is tied to ecology.

6. Human overpopulation has made the scope of the environmental problems unprecedented in human history, and we must address this problem.

The work is extensive, with many facets. The liabilities are countless, the rewards boundless. Enormous environmental damage has been done, but much of the earth still functions. The situation hangs in the balance. Extraordinary possibilities for destruction or for renewal challenge dedicated Christians right now.

This is what the Lord says:
"In the time of my favor I will answer you,
.    and in the day of salvation I will help you;
I will keep you and will make you to be a covenant
        for the people,
to restore the land. *(Isa. 49:8)*

Isaiah states the promise of God's help and the assurance of God's intent in the day of salvation. This is a hope and help for Christians, an assurance that adds a spiritual dimension to the eco-crisis which is often missing in other groups.

Christians, awake! Join in God's work!

## Questions for Discussion

1. What environmental problems are apparent in your home? In your community? In your county and state?

2. Discuss the meaning of "subdue the earth." What challenges do we as Christians face in taking care of the earth?

3. What is the difference between Eastern meditation and Christian contemplation?

4. Is the earth sacred?

5. Discuss the various threads of Christian thought on the care of the environment—dominion of the earth; stewardship; partners with God; sacramental; scientific; prophetic.

6. What are the three reasons outlined in the text for taking care of the earth?

7. What is God's sovereign will concerning the environment? How should Christians further God's purposes for the earth?

8. Discuss the six points listed in the Christian call to action. Is the list complete?

# 14. What Christians Have to Offer

THE Creator molded a planet of great complexity and beauty. This planet is the arena where many of God's plans and purposes are being worked out. So much of that purpose is unknowable to our questioning minds, but one thing we do know: the arena itself is in our care. We also know from the Bible that the natural world is part of the salvation and redemption Jesus Christ brought to earth. And we know that the health and vigor of the creation is somehow linked to the vitality of our spiritual lives.

As Christians we have something special to offer the environmental movement—which should not stand apart from but be integral to our faith. We reach out to the natural world with a commitment to Jesus Christ. We are centered by Christian spiritual disciplines and use our gifts in service of God. We can serve the environment as well as the unsaved and oppressed by offering our faith, hope and, love.

## Faith

Our faith begins with belief in the Creator God. The Lord is sovereign over all the earth, the universe, God's creatures, and humankind.

> And I will . . . put breath and spirit in you, and you shall live; and you shall know, understand, and realize that I am the Lord [the Sovereign Ruler, calling forth loyalty and obedient service]. *(Ezek. 37:6, Amplified)*

The mountains, seas, deserts, plains, farms, cities; every tree, every bird, each blade of grass, each pebble on the shore; everything belongs to the Creator. Neither fate nor chance but the Lord God Almighty governs the earth.

> The earth is the Lord's, and everything in it,
>     the world, and all who live in it;
> for he founded it upon the seas
>     and established it upon the waters. *(Ps. 24:1-2)*

> For every animal of the forest is mine,
>     and the cattle on a thousand hills
> I know every bird in the mountains,
>     and the creatures of the field are mine.
>                           *(Ps. 50:10-11)*

> For the Lord is the great God,
>     the great King above all gods.
> In his hand are the depths of the earth,
>     and the mountain peaks belong to him.
> The sea is his, for he made it,
>     and his hands formed the dry land. *(Ps. 95:3-5)*

We have faith that God has a plan and purpose for the whole creation. Some of God's purposes for the earth we know. Through the earth God sustains us, gives us evidence of the Creator's hand, and offers us opportunity to reflect on God's glory. We trust that God's sovereign will prevails and that, as the Psalmist wrote, God's purposes will ultimately be accomplished.

> But the plans of the Lord stand firm forever,
>    the purposes of his heart through all generations.
> *(Ps. 33:11)*

We have faith that it is God's will for humankind to care for the earth. Though there is evil in the world, Scripture nowhere records that the original command to take care of the earth has been withdrawn or changed.

God's first gift to us was that we should rule the earth, even though the earth still belongs to God. Our rule is not absolute nor is it independent. Our work is one of participation; we are subordinates in God's rule. Our work is a divine gift, not a right.

Our faith includes the reconciliation of Jesus Christ that brought salvation to all humankind, a saving grace that includes the creation.

> With all wisdom and insight he has made known to us the mystery of his will according to his good pleasure that he set forth in Christ as a plan for the fullness of time, to gather up all things in him, things in heaven and things on earth. *(Eph. 1:8b-10, NRSV)*

Our faith includes the ministry of the Holy Spirit. The Spirit of God that "hovered over the waters" in the beginning is that same Spirit that renews the earth.

> When you send your Spirit . . . you renew the face of the earth. *(Ps. 104:30)*

That Spirit is available to Christians today as Helper, Comforter, and Enabler in carrying out the message of Christ on earth.

> . . . he saved us, not because of any works of righteousness that we had done, but according to his mercy, through the water of rebirth and renewal by the Holy Spirit. This Spirit he poured out on us richly through Christ our Savior. . . .
> I desire that you inist on these things, so that those who have come to believe in God may be careful to devote themselves to good works.
> *(Titus 3:5-6, 8, NRSV)*

The generous outpouring of the Spirit will enable us to devote ourselves to doing "what is good" in the environmental crises.

## Hope

The Christian faith offers hope for humanity.

> Blessed be the God and Father of our Lord Jesus Christ! By his great mercy he has given us a new birth into a living hope through the resurrection of Jesus Christ from the dead. *(1 Pet. 1:3, NRSV)*

The Christian faith offers hope for the natural world.

> You answer us with awesome deeds of righteousness,
>     O God our Savior,
> the hope of all the ends of the earth
>     and of the farthest seas. . . *(Ps. 65:5)*

Our Christian walk offers hope for the fulfillment of God's plans for the earth.

> To them God has chosen to make known . . . the glorious riches of this mystery, which is Christ in you, the hope of glory. *(Col. 1:27)*

We have hope in the promises of restoration, the future new heaven and new earth. We have hope because the prayer of Jesus included the creation.

> "Our Father in heaven,
>     hallowed be your name.
> Your kingdom come.
>     Your will be done,
>         on earth as it is in heaven. *(Matt. 6:9-10, NRSV)*

Our prayers for creation echo the prayer Jesus taught his disciples—"your will be done, on earth as it is in heaven."

## Love

> And now these three remain: faith, hope and love. But the greatest of these is love. *(1 Cor. 13:13)*

The source of love is God, for "God is love" (1 John 4:16). God's love was poured into the great creative work of all time, the work of which we are a part. That love permeates God's natural world, from the tiniest detail on a pinecone to the vast panorama of a desert landscape.

> The earth is filled with your love, O Lord. *(Ps. 119:64)*

We sense God's love in the unspoiled corners of the

natural world and in the outstretched hand of one person helping another. God's love moves us with the colors of an evening sunset and in the quiet solitude of a foggy dawn.

We define love as a tender and deep feeling of affection, an attachment or devotion to someone or something. God's love shows in a benevolent concern for humans and compassion for the creation. We return that love as devout attachment to God.

> Jesus replied: " 'Love the Lord your God with all your heart and with all your soul and with all your mind.' This is the first and greatest commandment. And the second is like it: 'Love your neighbor as yourself.' "
> *(Matt. 22:37-39)*

Love is the central attribute of God, and the most important thing we can reflect as Christians in the image of God. Paul defines love in vivid language:

> Love is patient, love is kind. It does not envy, it does not boast, it is not proud. It is not rude, it is not self-seeking, it is not easily angered, it keeps no record of wrongs. Love does not delight in evil but rejoices with the truth. It always protects, always trusts, always hopes, always perseveres. Love never fails.
> *(1 Cor. 13:4-8)*

Sharing the love of God is the greatest thing we have to offer the natural world. To what others may do for the environment out of necessity and common sense, we can add the motive of Christian love.

## Living the Gospel

Living the gospel is another way Christians can help the

environmental movement. If we truly had followed Jesus' teachings throughout the ages, the natural world and the earth's peoples would be in better condition.

The gospel lifestyle is one of sharing and concerned action. It is a lifestyle of obedience to God's call to service. The very love we receive as Christians we extend to others and to God's creation. When we extend Christian love to plants and animals, mountains and meadows, fields and forests, deserts and oceans, we honor God's first command to care for the creation.

Our obedience is a loving response to the God who is love. Our participation in caring for the natural world can strengthen our ties to the Creator and help to further the divine purposes for the earth.

Christian obedience is a key to the kingdom. Jesus said,

As the Father has loved me, so have I loved you. Now remain in my love. If you obey my commands, you will remain in my love, just as I have obeyed my Father's commands and remain in his love. I have told you this so that my joy may be in you and that your joy may be complete. *(John 15:9-11, NRSV)*

The joy of Jesus comes from our love and obedience, another assurance from Scripture that the work of the Lord is one of gladness. No wonder the creation is called to respond with praise to God! We can join in the work of earth stewardship knowing it is a ministry of praise.

## Questions for Discussion

1. Why is faith important to Christian action?
2. What are the possibilities of Christian hope?
3. What is special about Christian love?
4. How do we live the simple life, when to live without such things as a car could be anything but simple?

# 15. Implementing a Ministry of Praise

## *Basic Premise*

Christians are called to care for the earth. The Scriptures show us the importance of the natural world to God and the divine purposes. The basic premise of the Christian ministry of praise includes:

1. The Creator God owns the creation and is sovereign over all the earth.

2. God's gift to humankind was a vocation—that the people take care of the earth.

3. Humans occupy the key position in creation care. This includes (a) reaching *upward*, with ability to perceive God, to understand and accept the reconciliation of Jesus Christ, and to receive guidance by the Holy Spirit; and (b) reaching *outward* in Christian service to all of God's creation.

4. The natural world is included in the salvation and redemption Jesus Christ brought to the earth.

5. The new life in Christ starts at the moment of salvation, therefore our fulfillment and joy in service begins here and now.

6. Social justice is inseparable from justice to the creation.

7. Because the condition of the earth is linked to the condition of our spiritual lives, we will commit or recommit our lives to Jesus Christ. This is a nonnegotiable commitment given by each person. When we are committed to or renewed in our belief, anything that follows is not just a righteous exercise; it is an outpouring of love and action in accordance with the Creator's plan.

8. As the fellowship of believers, we will continue in Christian worship, prayer, study, and fellowship.

The Scriptures are filled with the stories of the people God sent to fulfill divine purpose. These people felt inadequate, untrained, and weak, but they were *willing*. God strengthened and empowered them through the Holy Spirit to accomplish given tasks.

". . . I make known the end from the beginning
    from ancient times, what is still to come
I say: My purpose will stand,
    and I will do all that I please.
From the east I summon a bird of prey,
    from a far-off land, a man to fulfill my purpose.
What I have said, that I will bring about;
    what I have planned, that will I do."
                                        *(Isa. 46:10-11, NIV)*

Christians strive to become more like the image of God, so the ministry will be an outreach of God's love. Yet we are also expected to use all the abilities and strength that we have, for they are God-given too.

## What Do We Want?

Ecologists traverse the globe, studying the systems and creatures of the natural world. That knowledge gives us a basis from which to work. It has led us to realize how the earth works as a whole.

We know that seeding rainclouds for one area steals moisture from another. Cutting trees because they use water means less water storage. Trampling plants in the desert means they cannot hold their own during the inevitable drought. The extinction of one species of plant or animal signals that something is seriously wrong with the habitat. The interrelationships are endless and endlessly important.

Ultimately what we want for the environment is a continuing equilibrium of the dynamic system that shapes the workings of the earth, so that God's purposes for earth may be fulfilled. To achieve this, Christian environmentalists identify four objectives—sustainability, sufficiency, participation, and unity.

• **Sustainability.** As people of the earth, we must respect the integrity of the natural world. This is necessary so that natural systems continue to function properly and the beauty of the earth and its fruitfulness are maintained for all earth's creatures, human and nonhuman.[1] We must not interfere with the earth's ability to sustain its own systems.

As a society we must satisfy our needs without jeopardizing the prospects of future generations. Each generation must ensure that the next one inherits an undiminished natural and economic endowment.[2] We must not use more than our share. Indeed, we must conserve and nurture resources for the future, just as we put money in the bank as a hedge against unforeseen demands.

• **Sufficiency.** The earth provides sustenance for all, plants and animals alike, including humans. The norm of sufficiency would guarantee that every living creature would have sufficient means or resources to support life and health. Basic needs are minimum guarantees. These subsistence needs include food, water, shelter, clothing, medicines, and household fuel.

Christians know there is more to a person than a mouth to be fed or a body to be warmed. Basic needs include those capabilities which we develop to be in the image of God. These gifts include the ability to create; to relate lovingly and deeply to friends, parents, and children; to care for the natural world; and to serve God.[3] Humans need spiritual, educational, cultural, aesthetic, and leisure-time enrichment. These are the very foundations of human civilization.

Guaranteeing sufficiency for all makes us acutely aware that the good things of God's creation are to be shared. And this sharing must take place according to a keen and responsible sense of what is needful.[4] Separating our wants from our needs should not send us into a new and forbidding legal system, but should acknowledge the differences between individuals. A variety of social and cultural considerations enter into the assessments of what is required.

If Christians lead the way with a lifestyle of simplicity, much of the materialism of the twentieth century will be curtailed, and the resources we recover can be redistributed or used in more productive ways. A lifestyle of simplicity does not have to be one of grim austerity and deprivation. It is a lifestyle of *enough*.

Therefore do not worry, saying, "What will we eat?" or "What will we drink?" or "What will we wear?" For it is the Gentiles who strive for all these things: and indeed your heavenly Father knows that you need all these things. But strive first for the kingdom of God and his righteousness, and all these things will be given to you as well. *(Matt. 6:31-33, NRSV)*

This passage from Matthew gives us our priorities. First we seek God's kingdom, then we can work out the needs. As we struggle with daily decisions perhaps the bottom line is Larry Rasmussen's suggested question: "If my (our) standard of living were adopted by the whole world, would nature still flourish?" [5]

• **Participation.** In a productive natural system, every living thing plays some role or performs some function that helps sustain life and the environment. Every living creature participates.

Our dominion of the earth under God's rule is also a vocation of participation. Our work as subordinates under divine authority is a gift, one given to all humans.

A just economic system for humanity requires that there be opportunity for all to obtain and enjoy nature's sustenance. If some people are left out, something is wrong.[6] If individuals are denied participation in the economy because of unemployment, discrimination, the politics of power, they are denied freedom to exercise their gifts on behalf of themselves and others. This skews the dynamics of a cooperative system. The poor, the oppressed, the disadvantaged are likely to remain so unless we include them in economic plans and the concurrent work on the environment.

The Christian viewpoint validates the worth of the individual. This includes the expectation that all will be enabled to participate in an economic system that benefits everyone while sustaining the health of the environment.

• **Unity.** People are social beings. We live in community with one another and with our environment and its plants and animals. Living in community with one another assumes a common purpose for the good of all, a solidarity of thought and action that motivates and sustains the life of the group. This unity is not just an ideal to which we aspire, but a fundamental fact of the human condition.[7]

Spiritual unity in the early church brought about an extraordinary sharing fellowship.

> They devoted themselves to the apostles' teaching and fellowship, to the breaking of bread and the prayers.
> Awe came upon everyone, because many wonders and signs were being done by the apostles. All who believed were together and had all things in common; they would sell their possessions and goods and distribute the proceeds to all, as any had need. Day by day, as they spent much time together in the temple, they broke bread at home and ate their food with glad and generous hearts, praising God and having the goodwill of all the people. And day by day the Lord added to their number those who were being saved.
> *(Acts 2:42-47, NRSV)*

The sharing was a voluntary action, motivated out of love and in response to God's call. Such a response seems unattainable in our materialistic society. Yet this example can perhaps inspire us to examine our own response to God, as acted out in our homes and communities.

In the community of Christ, all members utilize their gifts for the common good. Thus the churches establish programs that call forth the gifts of the believers. The church validates those gifts, equips members for mission both within the church and beyond it, then supports its workers.

Such a model can be extended to the entire secular community, as we join forces to save the earth. Our interdependence and the Christian values we find in environmental work can help bring the unity that binds all endeavors for the common good. We can laugh and cry, pray and worship, plan and evaluate, share defeats and victories as we engage in the struggle. Any risk and uncertainty will be easier to cope with because of the cooperation and support we can offer each other.

The regional community can never be isolated, however, from the rest of the world. We know from our ecological studies that the blessings and problems of life on earth are global as well as regional. Therefore, we must stand with our neighbors, offering a helping hand and expertise across international borders, seeking the solidarity of world community. We share a common future.

## Goals

With environmental considerations in mind, Christians can formulate goals to focus the ministry of praise. Those goals should include:

1. Spreading the love of God to all of God's abundant creation by caring for the plants, animals, and the physical environment that supports all life.

2. Spreading the love of God to all the people of the earth. This includes bringing the news of a living, compassionate God who is personal, and conveying the great good news of the gospel of Jesus Christ.

3. Working toward the equilibrium of a dynamic biological system by healing the earth and establishing (a) sustainability, (b) sufficiency, (c) participation, and (d) unity throughout the creation.

4. Overcoming the debts and handicaps we face by (a)

unifying Christians in this ministry; (b) wiping out the environmental debt through the hard work of restoration; and (c) working to change the people's values from a materialistic lifestyle to one of simplicity.

5. Working with a gentle spirit as Jesus indicated. This entails an attitude of strength without aggression, firmness without an argumentative spirit. It implies a knowledge about the environment. It requires that Christians be filled with love as we go about doing the Lord's work.

6. Maintaining the environment with an attitude of integrity for life on earth—using but not abusing, enjoying without destroying—so the earth may become a place of praise to God.

## Evaluating Our Work

To know how we are doing, some means of assessing the work is necessary. After establishing specific environmental goals for a given area, a time should be established for measuring progress. Observation, tabulating test results, and even before-and-after comparisons can be helpful in evaluating whether a project is completed, or whether new efforts must be made to finish the work.

Human rating scales can tell us how well, what kind, or how many, and are useful. However, these devices are always geared to human standards. As Christians, we have something simpler and better.

## The Divine Standard

When God created the earth, a divine standard was set. We have an *absolute* to judge by. The Creator was and is loving, faithful, righteous, merciful, just, and holy. Paradise was good, beautiful, and functioned as an abundant and unified whole.

He has made everything beautiful in its time.

*(Eccl. 3:11)*

When we heal the earth, one of the fruits of that healing is a new sense of beauty.[8] As soon as we begin to deal with nature as we should, the beauty of nature will be restored and preserved. And not only beauty, but economic and human value will increase as the problems of ecology diminish.

It is an old saying that we should aim at the target we wish to hit. And perhaps the simplest target for us in environmental work is to once more beautify the earth. With God's guidance we can help in refurbishing the earth into a beautiful place more like the garden of Eden.

> They will say, "This land that was laid waste has become like the garden of Eden." . . . I the Lord have spoken it, and I will do it. *(Ezek. 36:35-36)*

The ultimate evaluation standards of goodness and beauty were shaped in heaven and for us are probably never wholly attainable. But the standards do give us something to strive for here on earth. When we have restored everything to its proper place, when living habitats and ecological communities are functioning well, when humankind is living in community with a certain abundance, then we can assess the work. Our criteria are simple: Is it good? Is it beautiful?

## *How Do We Accomplish Our Goals?*

### Organizing the Work

The game plan will be as diversified as the problems, situations, talent, and commitment available in any given locality. Christian groups organizing for the environmental work need to involve the people and assess the mission.

• **The Creation Keepers.** First, gather a group of caring people, sounding a call through the Christian community. Meeting to share concerns and interests can be the start of a local mission group. A Christian group will commit to prayer and Bible study as part of the sharing. Discovering and evoking the gifts of the members is important to the fulfillment of each person in ministry and to the group function. Uncovering the talents of the group may also have some bearing on the direction of the mission of earth stewardship.

• **The Mission.** As the group shares concerns for the environment, many needs will be identified. Using good problem-solving techniques, the group can set priorities; discuss problems; identify resources, needs, and required information; assess people-power; develop solutions; and outline strategies.

Matching the talents in the group to the tasks at hand is the logical way to approach the work. Another way is to encourage those with special concerns or interests. The added enthusiasm generates a lot of energy. Some jobs no one wants to do. The obvious plan then is for everyone to help.

An important part of the mission will be educational—spreading useful and needed information about recycling, reforesting, or new lifestyles. Political action will be the arena for some motivated persons, who might join local environmental action groups. Healing the environment by reclaiming spoiled habitat may involve others. Working person-to-person with the oppressed and poor, including them in environmental commitment, is also part of the ministry of compassion toward the earth.

The mission groups can operate within the church or beyond. Some projects may be so extensive that the call can be sounded in other churches. Citywide interdenominational groups may be needed for citywide projects.

Further inspiration about local mission groups can be gleaned from the writings of Elizabeth O'Connor, who chronicles the work of The Church of the Saviour in Washington, D.C. This congregation has functioned as a community of Christ for many years, initiating, developing, and refining the model of local mission groups.[9]

## Lessons from Scripture

Although the Holy Bible is not an ecology book, it is possible to find in its pages a few guidelines for our ministry of praise. Here are eight lessons from Scripture.

### 1. Stewards in God's Image:

> When God created humankind he made them in the likeness of God. Male and female he created them, and he blessed them. . . . *(Gen. 5:1-2, NRSV)*

In the image of God we walk the earth, and in that image we reflect the love, creativity, and caring for order and justice with which the Creator endowed the earth. In that image we act as earth stewards.

### 2. Study the Natural World:

> Great are the works of the Lord;
> They are studied by all who delight in them.
>
> *(Ps. 111:2, NASB)*

Since the Bible is not a science textbook, there are many things about earth stewardship it does not say. For example, it does not say we should recycle garbage or neutralize toxic waste. Nor does it give directions for planting a tree. For such knowledge we use our own experience, brains, and abilities.

The best way we can learn about the earth is to study it. Then we can approach earth ministry with the knowledge needed to live within the earth's dynamic system. Our study must be done with common sense and compassion. Unlike the graduate student who cut down the oldest living bristlecone pine and hauled it back to civilization in his pickup truck so he could study it, our techniques must neither destroy nor disrupt the environment.

Trained scientists tell us many of the earth's secrets, but anyone can profitably begin a study of nature. Becoming familiar with the plants and animals of our immediate surroundings is an undertaking of delight. That familiarity helps us feel at home in our own environment, strengthening our ties to the natural world.

Bringing the natural world closer can be beneficial. Seeding local wildflowers into the front lawn area reduces the need for excessive watering and mowing and attracts birds. Although it is not good to feed wild animals to the point of making them totally dependent on humans, it is a joy to watch them in backyard sanctuaries.

Studying God's creation is especially appropriate to Christian school curriculums. Science programs can be costly, but the importance to Christians of the knowledge and understanding of the environment should make science education a priority. Christians sometimes are wary of scientific thinking, but God has withstood the onslaught of scrutiny for many centuries.

Christian teachers can impart the wonder of the Lord's creation, letting students examine the design and discover the harmonies that unfold in the natural world. The more we know about the natural world, the more we know about God.

Christian schools have the opportunity to teach students to love the world that God made. When we love something, we tend to honor it and take care of it.

### 3. God Planted a Garden:

Now the Lord God had planted a garden in the east, in Eden; and there he put the man he had formed. And the Lord God made all kinds of trees grow out of the ground—trees that were pleasing to the eye and good for food. *(Gen. 2:8-9)*

We follow God's example when we plant a garden. The garden can be as simple as a few summer vegetables in a planter or as elaborate as the landscaping of a city park. Apartment dwellers can find a spot for a potted plant or two. Every plant is a plus for our immediate welfare, bringing not only beauty but refreshing the air and keeping us in more direct touch with God's creation.

If we considered our cities as gardens, we would find delight in replacing acres of asphalt and cement with trees, shrubs, and flowers. What a natural wonderland a city could be!

Saint Francis envisioned more. He said that when we consider the whole world a garden, then it will become an Eden, and give us everything we seek—bread and peace.[10]

### 4. God Maintained Wilderness:

He led you through the great and terrible wilderness, with its fiery serpents and scorpions and thirsty ground where there was no water; He brought water for you out of the rock of flint.

"In the wilderness He fed you manna which your fathers did not know, that He might humble you and that He might test you, to do good for you in the end."

*(Deut. 8:15-16, NASB)*

God also maintained wild gardens, which became places of prayer and sanctuary. The Lord used wilderness to build character and spiritual values in his people.

In the same way, wild areas preserve and promote healthy and vigorous plants and animals. This wide diversity of life is an important biological feature which preserves genetic variability. The plants and animals that survive in these areas are hardy specimens able to withstand seasonal extremes and adapt to changing environments. We might consider wilderness areas as storehouses for living varieties, a "talent pool" of plants and animals that sustains itself.

Even though we once thought of wilderness as an obstacle to civilization, it is now clear that large areas of wild country need to be preserved. These preserves will not truly be preserves unless they are maintained without the intrusive activities of mining and other developments, without sheep or cattle grazing, without feral animals. Domestic animals allowed to run loose and overgraze have caused the destruction of much good land and increased the number and extent of the world's deserts.

## 5. Noah Saved the Animals and the Food Supply:

You are to bring into the ark two of all living creatures, male and female, to keep them alive with you. . . . You are to take every kind of food that is to be eaten."

*(Gen. 6:19, 21)*

Noah might be considered the first conservationist. Trusting God, he built an ark on dry ground, preparing for the deluge. God directed him to save the animals and the food supply that would sustain them.

With the environment threatened and species of animals dwindling, it is time to follow Noah's example, but with a major difference—we should consider the whole planet an ark. Restoring habitats, reestablishing animal species in given areas, and using zoos to promote breeding of endangered species are some of the ways ecologists are improving and extending life for animal populations.

**6. Living the Gospel Lifestyle:**
Do not store up for yourselves treasures on earth.
*(Matt. 6:19)*

And he said to them, "Take care! Be on your guard against all kinds of greed; for one's life does not consist in the abundance of possessions." *(Luke 12:15, NRSV)*

Command those who are rich in this present world not to be arrogant nor to put their hope in wealth, which is so uncertain, but to put their hope in God, who richly provides us with everything for our enjoyment. Command them to do good, to be rich in good deeds, and to be generous and willing to share. *(1 Tim. 6:17-18)*

Keep your lives free from the love of money and be content with what you have, because God has said,
  "Never will I leave you;
  never will I forsake you." *(Heb. 13:5)*

These four passages warn us to beware of wealth and possessions. They direct us toward a life of simplicity, the lifestyle of the gospel. However, according to Paulos Mar Gregorios, "Simplicity of life is a high value, but enforced poverty is not."

Gregorios reminds us that Christians can choose from two lifestyles. First is the simple life of John the Baptist, who lived on locusts and honey in the desert. Second is the fuller life of our Lord, who prayed all night and worked all day, but who also ate and drank with others.

Neither of these lifestyles justifies the "mindless affluence" of our consumer society.[11]

Simplicity is needed to counteract the ongoing materialism of our culture, a materialism too easy to absorb and live. We know there are limits to the earth's resources; we can choose to set limits on personal use of these resources. The guidelines for earth management can be applied to our own situation. They include sustainability, sufficiency, participation, and unity.

The questions we ask ourselves might be these: What does it take to sustain this household without overusing the resources? What is sufficient to provide a decent and productive quality of life for every person in the household? Will everyone be insured of participation? Will this lifestyle help to unify us as a family, as the people of God?

We measure our needs against those of others and the environment. Our measuring cup cannot contain an excess of material wealth, yet should hold plenty for individual needs.

## 7. A Time for Rest:

By the seventh day God had finished the work he had been doing; so on the seventh day he rested from all his work.                                          *(Gen. 2:2)*

For six years you are to sow your fields and harvest the crops, but during the seventh year let the land lie unplowed and unused. Then the poor among your people may get food from it, and the wild animals may eat what they leave. Do the same with your vineyard and your olive grove.

Six days do your work, but on the seventh day do not work, so that your ox and your donkey may rest . . . and the alien as well, may be refreshed.

*(Exod. 23:10-12)*

God's rule provides for a time of rest. This rest extends to the land under cultivation, calling for fields to lie fallow every seventh year. This practice is still found to be beneficial to the soil, and good farmers rotate field crops from area to area, giving rest to the land.

Rest for the workers, the animals, and all of God's people is also good practice. We follow God's example by providing a day when we suspend our activities to find respite from labor, and time for worship, reflection, and leisure.

**8. The Christian Campaign:**
Blessed are the gentle, for they shall inherit the earth.
*(Matt. 5:5, NASB)*

With this simple directive, Jesus projected a quiet campaign. Those who truly inherit the land are not neighbors who quarrel over boundaries, nor nations that fight to extend borders. A gentle and humble attitude is the right approach, the result of an inner faith and confidence.

Achieving the Creator's plans and purposes for the earth requires an inner conviction that is lived out in a moderate lifestyle. That conviction will spark a willingness to replant the earth and restore the creation. Inner conviction will fuel the persistence needed to tolerate short-term loss for long-term gain, as we repay our debt to the environment and invest in the future of life on earth.

## *Where Do We Start?*

We start where we are. Faced with the dilemmas of the eco-crisis, the Christian will do best to start on the inside, assessing our personal strengths and weaknesses in terms of talent and spiritual growth. Then we will need to identify the places where we can engage in stewardship.

## Inward Assessment

For the Christian steward the beginning of any mission is spiritual grounding—digging into God's Word. We spend time reflecting, communicating with the Creator through prayer and Christian meditation and listening for guidance. Guidance is essential so that we do not run ahead of the Spirit, but do the right thing at the right time and in the right place.

The parable of the talents (Matt. 25:14-28) should be part of our reflection. We need to be sure where our talents lie, so that we use them to the glory of the Lord. Part of that discovery entails feedback and confirmation from a Christian sharing group, for sometimes we do not see ourselves with enough objectivity.

The man who received five talents put his money to work and gained five more. The Master rewarded him and invited him to share in the Master's joy. The man who received two talents gained two more. The Master rewarded him also and invited him to share the Master's joy. The two who gained much by their work and prudent investment were rewarded with more.

The man who had received only one talent hid it in the ground, then returned it to the Master. The Master was displeased and took it back. The servant was thrown outside "into the darkness."

The term *talent* in biblical times meant a unit of weight or coinage, and our present use of the word talent is derived from this parable. The metaphor still holds. If we assess our talents and spiritual gifts and put them to work in personal ministries, we will be following the plan of the Creator. For God gave us these abilities, and we are accountable for them.[12] When we use them in God's service, we find fulfillment in the work and share in the joy of the Master.

We need to leave room for the development and training of God-given talents, but that does not mean we have to delay serving others or the creation. Christians are always training for future work. In the meantime, God can use us where we are and as we are.

From our inward assessment, we establish ways to grow in Christ and practice the spiritual disciplines. We also identify our strengths and weaknesses. We discover our gifts, pinpoint our particular interests, and lay them before God in prayer. Then we are ready as the people of God to move into training and service.

## Outward Assessment

Assessing the outward mission as stewards of the creation calls for a realistic view of the scene. Environmental problems are extensive. The work involves moving people to a new way of life as well as undertaking special projects.

We begin with some handicaps. They include the burden of environmental debt; prevalence of a materialistic lifestyle; too many people; and a lack of unity on the part of Christians concerning this call to earth stewardship. What better way to challenge ourselves as we move into this blessed ministry!

• **Handicap: Environmental Debt.** The national debt of any given country is dwarfed by the enormous debt that twentieth-century humans have incurred in the environment. The results of that debt can be seen in wasted land, piles of garbage, denuded mountain slopes, spent mines, fouled air, and clogged waterways. These are areas of the planet that are unusable, polluted, barren, or unable to support life.

In the past two hundred years of industrial development, our extravagant and wasteful use of resources, both renewable and nonrenewable, have produced a staggering burden. We have pillaged and looted the earth out of greed and ignorance. In terms of using the earth's resources, we are heavily in debt to the future. The red ink runs on the balance sheet, as unmistakable as a dying, stinking river.

The environmental debt is a handicap in achieving the optimum balance quickly. We will have to tighten our belts while we restore and reshape the environment, for the earth cannot continue to support our wasteful and neglectful way of life.

In the long run, when we are in better balance with the environment, people may be able to live with a certain abundance. But until we repay our environmental debt and preserve life resources for the future, we must be willing to suffer short-term loss for long-term gain.

• **Handicap: A Materialistic Lifestyle.** The materialism of our present Western culture is a daily hindrance to living more simply. We constantly face decisions about what we need and what is sufficient.

One hour spent reviewing television commercials will expose the problem. The resources and energy spent on developing new fashions, trends, and products for every aspect of life are only part of the trouble. Many resources are also spent on marketing, packaging, and retailing. The results are often unnecessary buying and wasteful packaging as well as irresponsible attitudes on the part of the public, since buying trendy products fuels the desire for more.

Impulse buying saps our resources and hurts the environment. Distorted values warp our holidays and special occasions. The Christian family must find the discipline to establish a lifestyle of simplicity, set priorities, and educate every member of the family as to how simplicity works in everyday living.

Business at its best is a social service, providing needed goods and services to people. Businesses that are environmentally responsible engage in a good work.

• **Handicap: Overpopulation.** Runaway numbers of people now inhabit the globe. They make demands on the environment, trample the plants that sustain them, and elbow each other out of the way in the marketplace. Overcrowding brings on emotional and social problems by sheer weight of numbers. The earth itself is over-developed to fill desire for living space. Water becomes scarce, the skies more polluted, and food limited. The earth cannot sustain too many people.

Many countries are working to solve this problem. It requires responsible citizens and a network of health education and family planning resources. It would be unfortunate to have to legislate solutions to overpopulation. The human family is the core of community, and children and old people are to be cherished. Yet the crush of people that inhabit this planet is exacerbating the environmental destruction.

In his essay, "Invitation to Wonder: Toward a Theology of Nature," Robert Meye reminds us that increase for us in the present may mean the death of our brother or sister in the future.[13] There is need for responsible and informed Christian work in this area.

• **Handicap: Problems Within the Christian Community.** Worshiping, praying, and working with fellow Christian hold some of the joys of the new life in Christ. The focus of Christianity brings us together. But because we are human, we are not always of one mind. We come from varied backgrounds, with diverse training, and we are in different stages of spiritual growth. The differences of opinion, misunderstandings, ignorance, and misconceptions of what we are about seem inevitable.

Concerning the importance of God's creation, the body of Christ has been caught napping. The environmental movement started outside the church. As this book tries to show, our faith heritage is rich in concern for the environment. But messages from the pulpit about God's creation have been rare, and environmental action has not been a common outreach of the church.

Now as the church scrambles for a theology of the environment, it is time to check our assumptions about the natural world and our religion. Some Christians:

1. Think the Old Testament Scriptures have all been changed or superseded by the New Testament. In Matthew 5:17, Jesus reminded his disciples that he had not come to abolish the law or the prophets, but to fulfill them.

2. Think that God will take care of everything. In Romans 8:28 we read that those who love God have been called according to his purpose. Philippians 2:13 says God works in us to will and to act according to his good purposes.

3. Believe there will be a new heaven and new earth, so we don't have to worry about this one. In Psalm 8:6-8 the psalmist reminds us the God gave us the care of the earth and its creatures.

4. Think the second coming of Christ is imminent, so why worry about things like automobile smog devices? In Acts 1:7 we read that we will not know the times or dates that God has set, but we will be witnesses for Christ to the ends of the earth.

5. Would rather argue about evolution than care for God's creatures. In Genesis 1:26 humans are given rule over the fish of the sea, birds of the air, livestock, all the earth, and all creatures that move along the ground.

6. Would rather argue about details of doctrine than be about the business of Christian ministry, including earth stewardship. Titus 3:9 warns against foolish controversies, genealogies, arguments and quarrels about law, because they are unprofitable and useless.

In terms of earth stewardship, Scripture provides one difficult passage—2 Peter 3:5-11. Peter's statement that the earth will be destroyed is hard to explain. This passage has been a battleground between some interpreters. The translation of some phrases is ambiguous.[14] The language is figurative.[15] The time frame is God's.[16]

It seems unlikely that one passage would negate all the other Scriptures which show the close association found between the natural world and God's plans, purpose, and arena for human spiritual growth. Without arguing the validity of one interpretation over another, it seems more to the point to consider Peter's subsequent question and answer: "What kind of people ought you to be? You ought to live holy and godly lives as you look forward to the day of God and speed its coming" (2 Pet. 3:11-12).

As outlined in *The Interpreter's Bible*, Peter is trying to indicate

> how a Christian should live in an age which expects such a glorious—and awful—conclusion. Surely he must live a spiritually prepared life. He ought also to live in an expectant mood as he waits and works for new heavens and a new earth in which righteousness dwells. He ought to be a person of integrity, a man of peace who acquiesces in the will of God, ever on his guard lest he be taken in by the error of lawless men and lose [his] stability in the truth.[17]

The will of God on the subject of earthkeeping was simply stated in Genesis. With that in mind, we have to ask ourselves some hard questions.

If God told us to take care of the earth in the very beginning, why are we not doing so?

If the creation is one major way the Creator is revealed, why are we allowing it to be ruined?

If the earth is the location God has chosen, are we going to help destroy it before God's plan is accomplished?

When judgment day comes, are we going to present the Lord with an earth that is a total wreck?

If we think this earth will pass away, in all its goodness and beauty, is there not one person who will intervene and speak for the earth?

Scripture tells us over and over that the Lord loves the earth and its inhabitants. God has given us every chance to return to him. We have every assurance that the Lord hears prayer. Who knows? If we petition on behalf of this beautiful planet, the Lord just might be waiting to respond.

## The Field

The field for environmental ministry lies wherever we happen to be, for we all live on this planet. Individual concerns start within our own households, where we take up the tasks of recycling, replanting, conserving energy and water, and the myriad other activities that will reshape the way we live.

Christians also join in community, state, and national efforts to make sensible and informed decisions about the use of natural resources and the efficiency of our life-support systems. A Spirit-led, informed Christian has the opportunity to represent a balanced viewpoint in these important matters.

Many Christians have already joined political action groups and environmental campaigns to stop abuses of the environment. Other Christians are committed to the education side of the problem. They are working on re-educating people to better ways of living and conserving to preserve the environment and preserve life. Church fellowship groups have gathered litter along designated stretches of highways, and youth groups have joined with the Forest Service in planting trees.

In addition to these projects, so important in the battle

to reclaim the earth, we must not overlook the immediate sphere of operation and influence that Christians groups have in church-owned lands and properties. Church buildings and property, camp and conference grounds, environmental impact of church fellowship groups, and missionary outreach are a particular stewardship responsibility.

• **The Church.** When the body of Christ meets to worship, work, study, pray, and fellowship, it has an impact on the environment. As a group we consume energy, food, and material objects and are often as wasteful as the society we live in, producing garbage while doing good works. We control considerable real estate, lands, and buildings that are often lacking care and good management. In short, as the body of Christ we are running up our own environmental debt.

Church members who still use Styrofoam cups for coffee hour should be aware that if they sailed from Hawaii to California, about a five-day adventure, they would seldom be out of sight of Styrofoam or other plastic floating in the water. Christians on holiday who carry six-packs of soft drinks should know that in a cleanup of the beach at Long Beach, California, literally thousands of plastic rings that hold the six-pack cans were picked up in one day. The impact of fun on the environment can be devastating.

Making the church environmentally aware is a step in the right direction. Serious discussion of problems and solutions will trigger action, for people want to do the right thing. Caring for the creation can easily be incorporated into the workings of the church. Then as we move into the outer community, we set an example of Christian stewardship.

• **Church Buildings.** Maintenance is no longer enough. Church buildings need to be made energy efficient with insulation, window coverings, and energy-saving air-conditioning and heating systems. New churches can be designed or old churches redesigned to take advantage of solar energy. The list of ways to improve energy consumption is limited only by the creativity and resourcefulness of the buildings and grounds committees.

• **Church Land.** The care of church grounds and property is usually delegated to volunteer labor. If the commitment fails, the grounds show the neglect. But if we are really serious about restoring the beauty of the earth and taking care of the land, this extra chore for church members can become a labor of love and outreach.

We can make the grounds pleasing with plantings and energy-efficient watering systems. Some churches have space for prayer gardens and could establish a quiet outdoor spot for moments of retreat. Other churches have enough land that it could be cultivated, providing garden space for the disadvantaged, a ministry in itself.

• **Camps and Conference Grounds.** Retreat properties that are locations for Christian camps and conference centers are often neglected sites in terms of healthy plant and animal populations. They are too often crammed with buildings and playing fields. The staff is seasonal, and there is no overall conservation nor appreciation plan. Those very sites need to be managed and conserved as the showcase of the Creator God. It is in the beauty of the natural world that many non-Christians are first moved to seek the living and personal God of the universe.

The specific goal of Christian camps is to bring individuals to the saving grace of Jesus Christ, to renew the spiritual life of the saints, and to equip them for service. As vital as that is to the Christian walk, we should not forget the peripheral teachings we instill at the same time. Appreciation for the Lord's creation and a stewardship of the earth are two such teachings.

Christian camps are usually in excellent locations for

teaching Christians about the environment and importance of earth stewardship. If a camp recycles garbage, that
sets an example to follow. If the camp works to conserve
energy, preserve the immediate environment, and promote the care of creation, the camper will take notice. If
camp improvement projects include caring for trees and
other plants, maintaining trails and waterfront areas, and
preserving some areas for quiet solitude, then campers begin to change their attitude toward the environment.

People want to feel at home in the outdoors, and the
only way to accomplish that is to establish a great familiarity with the natural world. That means learning the names
of plants and animals, learning the habitat areas, observing
the movement of birds and others animals, learning the
geologic formations, identifying rocks and minerals, experiencing the very landscape through hikes and walks, or
following creeks to the source to investigate the mystery of
springs. A Christian naturalist can supply this information.

An indispensable staff member, the Christian naturalist can help lay the groundwork for knowing God. The creation is the ultimate teaching tool, awakening in the unbe-
liever the concept of a personal, caring Creator God, the
one who promises salvation. Because of their unique locations, the possibilities are limitless for Christian camps
with a heart for this ministry.

• **Missionaries.** Missionaries find that the creation is
often the key to introducing the message of redemption in
Jesus Christ. To convey the concept of a living Creator
God who is personal and caring, the story of the Creation
of the world is often told first, just as in the Bible. The
Psalms and other passages, telling of the beauty of the
earth and of the compassion of the Creator God, lead into
the sin of humankind and the need for salvation. Then the
hope of redemption in Jesus Christ becomes the great
good news.

Missionaries carry more than the gospel with them. They also carry cultural habits and behaviors, possibly including the wasteful ways and environmental ignorance of a twentieth-century technological society. A thoughtful review of the environmental needs can correct this. Other cultures need to be supported in established habits of sustaining the earth and educated to needed ways of preservation. They should be warned about our mistakes. Lifestyle changes should be tailored to fit the prevailing culture.

Ecological ignorance is not limited to the Western world. Humans everywhere need information, creative thinking, and technology to restore lands and find balanced ways of living. This kind of help needs to be part of our foreign outreach.

• **Women's Groups.** The women's groups of local churches are frequently the most stable groups within the church. They seem oblivious to the doctrinal or political storms that can sweep over a congregation and continue a quiet program of study and devotion.

Women's groups traditionally tend to the housekeeping of the church. They decorate pews and pulpits, raise monies for mission through bazaars that feature handmade crafts and goods, nourish educational programs, and tend needs in times of family emergencies.

Now feminist voices are reminding women of other roles in worship and voicing the unique perspective of women, including the plight of the poor and the damage to the environment. Many women's groups are devoted particularly to prayer. They sustain the spiritual life of the church through organized prayer efforts.

Rapid progress might be made in the ecology effort if Christian women focused their prayers on the problems of the environment and the poor, then turned their considerable management, housekeeping, and nurturing talents to cleaning up the earth. Christian women in the home still do most of the buying for the family, spearhead holiday celebrations, decorate the home, teach and convey social manners and customs. In short, they play a key role in maintaining the lifestyle of the family and therefore the culture. When women truly understand the environmental need for change, they will find themselves making changes in the home. As a result they will wield phenomenal influence for good on earth.

## How Do We Begin?

The outreach of the ministry of praise starts with a seed planted, a can recycled, a forest saved, a neighbor helped, a congressman lobbied, a petition signed, the gospel shared, the poor helped to plant a garden. The ways and means of stewardship fall into two categories.

• **Immediate Healing.** This includes all the glaring destruction that needs immediate attention. These are the problems that cannot wait. Nuclear waste, toxic dumping, air pollution, water pollution, and other obvious problems fall into this category. The source of the trouble must be dealt with, and the economic and social implications can be serious. Solutions may take concerned political awareness and compassionate action.

• **Healing for the Future.** Education is the key to long-term change. Learning and sharing new lifestyle habits are an ongoing project. Learning nature's ways as we become familiar with the great outdoors will help us better understand the creation. We will more fully appreciate the plants and animals we can identify and know about.

Serious study of the creation needs to continue. If biologists, naturalists, and ecologists give us the big picture, then nations can cooperate effectively. At the same time, scientists also teach us what will help our daily earthkeeping. The studies must be done responsibly. Research that brings suffering or destruction to God's creation should be called into question.

## The Christian Commitment

• **The Call.** Over long ages of time, living things have changed the face of the earth, enriching it, molding it, carving out habitats and biological areas that support abundant life. When compared to the size of the earth, this has occurred in a limited zone. The soil, usable water, and breathable air are contained in a narrow band of environmental resources that encircle the vast bulk of the planet.

We have fouled this band, interrupting systems, until we now see signs that the life-support systems are failing. The earth will undoubtedly survive this assault, but there is no guarantee for humanity nor for all of God's creatures. Survival is not the only goal, however. The quality of life could become so poor that life might not be worth living for many people.

The danger signals are up, but it is not too late. We can replant the earth, restore biological areas, replenish habitats, and nurture animal life. The work calls for a serious ministry to the earth. People are needed who will extend the love of God to the creation.

• **The Christian.** All Christians have a stake in preserving the environment, managing their own households in a responsible way, and supporting community efforts. Many will feel a particular call to earth stewardship, giving most of their time and energy to the ministry of praise.

Christians know that the Lord revealed himself in three ways—through the creation, the incarnation, and Scripture. Therefore Christians have a serious interest in protecting and disseminating the Scriptures, telling the truth about the incarnation of Jesus Christ, and preserving God's creation.

• **The Spiritual Disciplines.** The disciplines of the Spirit shape our inner life and nurture our Christian growth. Study, prayer, confession, worship, and the other forms of inward and outward discipline help center us in our lay ministries and must never be neglected.

Praying for our earth ministry will sustain us in the work and help us find the guidance we need. Prayer will show us the need for confession of our failure in taking care of the earth. The admission before God of that failure and our accompanying repentance for this neglect is surely needed. Only when we have God's forgiveness is the slate wiped clean so we can begin the work.

Guidance is what we seek. Yes, we do our part, with hard work, sweat, and even tears. But the initial guidance for the project comes from God. We can learn to listen to the Spirit. Some people think this is old-fashioned, and that we are on our own. But that is not what the Christian walk is all about.

Listening for the Spirit pulls us into closer communion with God and his intentions. The word of guidance sometimes comes through Scripture, sometimes through others, and for some through an inner conviction or insight. The ways of the Spirit are myriad, and when there is doubt, we have the checks and balances of Scripture and the counsel of prayer partners and fellow Christians.

• **The Charge.** The work of the great commission (Matt. 28:18-20) is twofold. We "go and make disciples of all nations." We also follow up by "teaching them to obey everything." Jesus' commands include obeying the Lord out of love. And the first command the Lord gave us was to care for the earth and all its creatures (Gen. 1:28).

The restoration and preservation of the natural world is the major engagement of the century. The environment supports every life, and every life should support the environment.

As Christians we can support the environment because we have a hope that fills us with discipline and purpose. We know that no matter what the situation at present, God's will for the earth and its creatures will prevail. God's purposes will be accomplished.

> For the earth will be filled with the knowledge of the
>    glory of the Lord,
> as the waters cover the sea. *(Hab. 2:14)*

As we look forward to that day, and speed its coming, we claim this promise of Habakkuk: that the world will be filled with the knowledge of the glory of the Lord.

Let it begin with us. We play a strong role in accomplishing God's purposes. We are the hands; we are the feet. God provides the setting, the opportunities, the guidance. We provide the hard work, maintaining the earth and preparing for the future. We must be about the Lord's business—earth stewardship, a ministry of praise.

## Questions for Discussion

1. Discuss the eight points of the basic premise for ministry to the earth. Is the list complete?

2. Consider the four ecological objectives for environmental work—sustainability, sufficiency, participation, and unity. How would these work for a given problem in your area?

3. Discuss the Christian goals for earth stewardship. How are they different from the ecological objectives?

4. With the divine standard of beauty in mind, take stock of your own home, neighborhood, church facilities, town or area. Are environmental problems linked to economic problems? What can be done about them?

5. Can you think of other lessons from Scripture that might be applied in environmental ministry?

6. Assess your own inner strengths and weaknesses. Think how you might use these in taking care of the Lord's creation.

7. How shall we overcome the handicaps to our ministry for a more beautiful earth? Can you do anything locally about the environmental debt, a materialistic lifestyle, overpopulation, or attitude problems of the Christian community?

8. Where does your local church stand in the environmental campaign? Can improvements be made in your church facilities, conference grounds, activities, or outreach?

9. How can Christians stay centered spiritually while pursuing an environmental ministry?

10. What makes an environmental ministry a ministry of praise?

## Prayer for the Earth

O Lord, Creator of the universe,
Hear our prayer.
We speak to you on behalf of the earth.
. . . the planet which you provided with abundant life
 and intricate forms of beauty,
This earth which you gave into our care and keeping.

We confess our failure to care for your creation.
We confess our fault in the destruction,
 the waste,
  the greed,
   the politics of power,
    the ignorance,
     the heedlessness
 that are ruining the earth . . .
Most of all we confess our separation from you, Lord.
We have not loved you enough,
We have not followed your ways.

Forgive us, Lord,
Take us once more into your loving arms.
We want to follow Jesus.
 Fill us with your Holy Spirit.
 Strengthen us for our ministry to each other and to the
  earth.
 Grant us your healing love as we minister to those who
  need help.
Bless our coming together as the community of Christ
 to meet in worship, study, fellowship, and sharing.
Bless the earth, Lord,
 and all its inhabitants.
Bless the abundance of life;
 may it thrive under our care.
Help us to accomplish all we can for you,
 in spreading the gospel,

in helping others,
in restoring and renewing the earth.
We claim your promise that the earth will be filled
with the knowledge of the Lord.
Send your peace with each dawn,
Be with us in a flowing love that marks our days,
Sit beside us in the beauty of your world.
When the color-drenched sun drops below the western
horizon,
When the mountains sing your praise,
When the lark lifts its voice to the sky,
Hear the singing that wells up from our hearts,
Hear the voices of the whole creation
in soaring, freely given harmony.

We long for your presence,
Walk once more in your gardens, Lord,
the gardens we prepare.
We wait,
we watch,
expectantly.
We love you, Lord.
In the name of Jesus. Amen.

O sing a new song to the Lord,
sing to the Lord all the earth. . . .
Give the Lord glory and power
Give the Lord the glory of his name. . . .
Worship the Lord in his temple.
O earth, tremble before him. . . .
Let the heavens rejoice and earth be glad,
let the sea and all within it thunder praise,
let the land and all it bears rejoice,
all the trees of the wood shout for joy
at the presence of the Lord.

*(Ps. 96:1, 7-9, 11-13)* [18]

# Notes

**Chapter 1**
1. Schaeffer, Francis A., *Pollution and the Death of Man: The Christian View of Ecology* (Wheaton, Ill.: Tyndale House Publishers, 1979), p. 38.
2. Monsma, John C., ed., *The Evidence of God in an Expanding Universe: Forty American Scientists Declare Their Affirmative Views on Religion* (New York: G. P. Putnam's Sons, 1958).

**Chapter 2**
1. Tenney, Merrill C., gen. ed., *The Zondervan Pictorial Encyclopedia of the Bible*, vol. 1 (Grand Rapids, Mich.: Zondervan Publishing House, 1986), p. 1023.

**Chapter 3**
1. Granberg-Michaelson, Wesley, *A Worldly Spirituality* (San Francisco: Harper & Row, 1984), p.141.
2. Schaeffer, p. 26.

**Chapter 4**
1. Marshall, Catherine, *The Helper* (New York: Avon Books, 1979).

2. Gaebelein, Frank E., ed., *The Expositor's Bible Commentary*, Regency Reference Library, vol. 6 (Grand Rapids, Mich.: Zondervan Publishing House, 1986), p. 208.

## Chapter 5
1. Gaebelein, p. 182.
2. Wilkinson, Loren, ed., *Earthkeeping* (Grand Rapids, Mich.: W.B. Eerdmans Publishing Co., 1980), p. 216.
3. Granberg-Michaelson, p. 94.

## Chapter 8
1. Granberg-Michaelson, p. 79.
2. Barker, Kenneth, p. 1325, n. 2:22.

## Chapter 9
1. Lockyer, Herbert, *All the Doctrines of the Bible* (Grand Rapids, Mich.: Zondervan Publishing House, 1964), p. 275.
2. Buttrick, George A., ed., *The Interpreter's Bible*, vol. 4 (Nashville, Tenn.: Abingdon Press, 1980), p. 782.
3. Lockyer, p. 276.
4. Granberg-Michaelson, p. 87.
5. Brundtland, Gro Harlem, chairperson, World Commission on Environment and Development, *Our Common Future* (Oxford: Oxford University Press, 1987), p. 37.
6. Unger, Merrill F., *Unger's Bible Dictionary* (Chicago: Moody Press, 1979), p. 841.
7. Granberg-Michaelson, p. 87.
8. Wilkinson, Loren, p. 237.
9. Ibid., p. 238.
10. Ibid., p. 239.
11. Ibid., p. 244.

## Chapter 10
1. Gaebelein, vol. 7, p. 254.
2. Gaebelein, vol. 6, p. 923.
3. Barker, p. 1717, n. 8:21.
4. Tenney, vol. 3, p. 771.

## Chapter 11
1. Marshall, Catherine, *Something More* (New York: McGraw Hill Co., 1974), p. 30.
2. *The Encyclopaedia Britannica*, vol. 16., Macropaedia (Chicago: Encyclopaedia Britannica, Inc., William Benton, pub., 1981), p. 791.

## Chapter 12
1. Postema, Don, *Space for God* (Grand Rapids, Mich.: Bible Way, 1983), p. 178.

## Chapter 13
1. Brundtland, p. 3.
2. Meyer, Art and Jocele Meyer, *Earthkeepers* (Scottdale, Pa.: Herald Press, 1991), p. 37.
3. *The Bethel Series*, p. 4.
4. Gregorios, Paulos Mar, "New Testament Foundations for Understanding the Creation," Wesley Granberg-Michaelson, ed., *Tending the Garden*, (Grand Rapids, Mich.: Wm. B. Eerdmans Publishing Co., 1987), p. 92
5. Rasmussen, Larry, "Toward an Earth Charter," *The Christian Century*, October 23, 1991, p. 965.
6. Ibid., p. 967.
7. Friesen, Garry, with J. Robin Maxson, *Decision Making and the Will of God* (Portland, Ore.: Multnomah Press, 1980), p. 213.
8. Hoffman, Mark S., ed., *The World Almanac and Book of Facts 1991* (New York: Pharos Books, Scripps Howard Co., 1990), p. 610.
9. Brand, Paul W., "A Handful of Mud," Granberg-Michaelson, ed., Tending the Garden, p. 148.

## Chapter 15
1. Presbyterian Eco-Justice Task Force, *Keeping and Healing the Creation* (Louisville, Kent.: Presbyterian Church (USA), 1989), p. 63.
2. Brown, Lester R., proj. dir., *State of the World 1990* (New York: W. W. Norton and Co., 1990), p. 174.
3. Wilkinson, p. 245.

4. Presbyterian Eco-Justice Task Force, p. 73.

5. Rasmussen, Larry L., "Creation, Church, and Christian Responsibility," Granberg-Michaelson, ed., *Tending the Garden,* p. 129.

6. Presbyterian Eco-Justice Task Force, p. 68.

7. Ibid., p. 76.

8. Schaeffer, p. 73.

9. O'Connor, Elizabeth, *Journey Inward, Journey Outward* (New York: Harper & Row, 1968).

10. Carretto, Carlo, *I, Francis* (New York: Orbis Books, Maryknoll, 1982), p. 79.

11. Gregorios, p. 92.

12. O'Connor, Elizabeth, *Eighth Day of Creation: Discovering Your Gifts and Using Them* (Waco, Tex.: Word Books, 1971), p. 15.

13. Meye, Robert P., "Invitation to Wonder: Toward a Theology of Nature," Granberg-Michaelson, ed., *Tending the Garden,* p. 46.

14. Gaebelein, vol. 12, p. 286.

15. Barker, p. 1903, n. 3:10.

16. Buttrick, George A., ed., *The Interpreter's Bible*, vol. 12, p. 198.

17. Ibid., p. 199.

18. Gelineau, Joseph, *The Psalms (Singing Version) A New Translation* (New York: Paulist Press, 1966), p. 170.

# Scripture Index

# Subject Index

Made in the USA
Coppell, TX
09 April 2020

19131804R00105